French in the Primary Classroom

Resources available for download

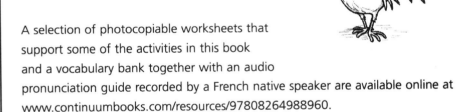

A selection of photocopiable worksheets that support some of the activities in this book and a vocabulary bank together with an audio pronunciation guide recorded by a French native speaker are available online at www.continuumbooks.com/resources/9780826498960.

Please visit the link and register with us to receive your password and access to these downloadable resources.

If you experience any problems accessing the resources, please contact Continuum at info@continuumbooks.com

Also available from Continuum

100 + Ideas for Teaching Languages, N. Griffith (2007)

Getting the Buggers into Languages, A. Barton (2006)

Teaching Foreign Languages in the Primary School, C. Kirsch (2008)

French in the Primary Classroom

Ideas and Resources for the Non-Linguist Teacher

Angela McLachlan

continuum

Continuum International Publishing Group
The Tower Building   80 Maiden Lane, Suite 704
11 York Road   New York,
London SE1 7NX   NY 10038

www.continuumbooks.com

© Angela McLachlan 2008

Angela McLachlan has asserted her right under the Copyright, Designs and Patents Act, 1988, to be identified as Author of this work.

First published 2008

British Library Cataloguing-in-Publication Data
A catalogue record for this book is available from the British Library.

ISBN: 9780826498960 (paperback)

Library of Congress Cataloging-in-Publication Data
McLachlan, Angela.
  French in the primary school : ideas and resources for the non-linguist teacher / Angela McLachlan.
     p. cm.
  ISBN 978-0-8264-9896-0 (pbk.)
  1. French language—Study and teaching (Primary)—English speakers. I. Title.
  PC2066.M45 2008
  372.65'41044—dc22

                                                    2008033579

Copyright Disclaimer
Every effort has been made to acknowledge copyright. Any omission is wholly unintended.

Illustrated by Clare Jarvis
Typeset by Ben Cracknell Studios | www.benstudios.co.uk
Printed and bound in Great Britain by Athenaeum Press Ltd., Gateshead, Tyne & Wear

Contents

Acknowledgements

A heartfelt thanks to all the teachers, pupils and colleagues who have given so willingly of their time, expertise, insight and wit!

Dedication

This book is of course dedicated to Harry, Marie, Bella and Fizz – the 'French is fun' four!

Introduction

Le français – c'est super!

For me, teaching languages in the primary school is first and foremost about engaging young children with learning, and French offers both teachers and pupils a wealth of opportunities for enhancing literacy, numeracy and thinking skills, as well as for embedding cross-curricular themes and links. Looking at the wider world, at how our neighbours live and speak, and thinking about how we might use language to communicate effectively, are an integral part of children's growing understanding of what it means to be a citizen of the world. What better way of doing that than through the lens of another language, and making friends with children further afield who speak that language?

Over the years, I've had lots of fun working with children and teachers, trying out new ideas and thinking carefully about what works, and what doesn't, and I have gathered some of them together here. This book is written for trainee and in-service primary teachers who may not have a great deal of experience in either speaking or teaching French. Remember, there is still a great deal you can do with even minimal language skills – French in the primary school is about literacy, oracy, intercultural understanding, knowledge about language and language learning strategies – skills which you are working on already through the Primary National Strategy.

French in the Primary Classroom provides ideas, games, activities, facts and information to get you started with French in the primary school . . . They are not aimed at any one particular year group – simply adapt them according to your pupils' ages and abilities. There are a number of photocopiable sheets to support some of the activities, and several more are available online www.continuumbooks. com/resources/97808264988960. To help with pronunciation and general vocabulary-building, a **bank of words** together with accompanying **sound files** recorded by a

French native speaker, my colleague Gaelle Flower, are also available to download:
www.continuumbooks.com/resources/97808264988960

Learning a new language is a journey into a new world for both teachers and pupils –
so, bon voyage!

Claude will be your guide

Allons-y!

Getting Started with French: Ideas for Planning, Teaching and Assessment

Length and structure of lessons

The first thing that needs to be decided on is the length of the French lessons. There are arguments for 'little and often' such as 15 minutes every two days, because it gives pupils more frequent exposure to language, and there is something to be said for a more lengthy weekly lesson, say 45 minutes, as this gives you time to combine a blend of activities that include speaking, listening, reading, and writing. I favour a lengthier lesson – and anything less than 45 minutes wouldn't count! A 15-minute slot does not lend itself particularly well to a real engagement with language.

It's generally unrealistic to expect that primary schools can provide two weekly 45-minute slots, so to ensure continuity in learning, embed French into your class homework diary, providing an opportunity for some out-of-school learning. Try to avoid cancelling French lessons – a gap of 14 days is a very long time in a young language learner's life!

Lessons work well when there is a blend of both language and cultural information, an opportunity for comparison with English, and group discussion – so don't worry if your French is somewhat rusty, you can use English too!

 Teaching tip

Write a letter to parents or guardians (chers parents et tuteurs) telling them that you're learning French – outline the kinds of things you might be doing, and the kinds of work the pupils might be bringing home – encourage them to help pupils with their homework, test them on their vocabulary quiz words and even learn a little French themselves.

The Qualifications and Curriculum Authority (QCA) Scheme of Work for French at KS2 is a good starting point (**www.standards.dfes.gov.uk/** or **www.qca.org.uk/qca_7055.aspx**). This will give you plenty of ideas about how you might structure your lessons, and the kind of language and cultural information you can include.

Employ a variety of activities, including whole-group, small-group and pair work. It's important to give pupils a chance to work by themselves too. I'd recommend you embed reading and writing from the very beginning, not only because some learners need to see the word before they can process it properly, but also because reading and writing are an integral part of language. Homework is an ideal opportunity for building up familiarity with the written word – moving from individual words to more complex sentences, and eventually short paragraphs, that can also act as a model for pupils to try out their own. Include some core language in every lesson, with some additional language to challenge more able pupils. Until you feel more confident, it helps to script a general outline of what you might say, and the kinds of things you'd like the pupils to say. Don't get tongue-tied in long complex sentences in French, keep things simple. Remember to start each lesson with a thorough recap of what you did in the previous lesson – get into the routine of a pupil having to describe the last lesson at the start of the next one, asking the whole class if anything has been missed out – if not, award a bonus point! As a plenary, ask pupils to summarize the key points of the lesson – warn them beforehand, so that they can pay particular attention, and do this on a rota basis, so that everyone has a go in the hot seat!

The three Ps of language teaching and learning: presentation, practice and production

Language teachers often talk in terms of the three Ps – presentation, practice and production – as the key steps towards ensuring pupils can learn, retain and ultimately be creative with, new language. When you begin to plan your French lessons, make sure that you are allocating sufficient time within individual lessons for each step – and keep providing opportunity for practice and production, both orally and in writing.

Presenting new language: key points

- Keep the amount of new language manageable, gradually building up vocabulary.
- Don't spend longer than 15 minutes presenting new language – give the pupils something to do with the language as soon as possible, in pairs or in small groups.
- Keep going back to words or sentences you're working on – don't move on too quickly.
- Use visual aids where you can – flashcards, mime, gesture, pictures, real objects (realia). When you're working with written texts, it's OK to include some unknown words to encourage pupils to think about the overall meaning the text is conveying.
- Always encourage pupils to listen, then repeat, very carefully, giving them lots of opportunity to play with the new word and its sound.
- Keep things relevant – if you're working on verbs, choose those that pupils actually do (or avoid doing!) like: jouer au foot, chanter, danser, aller à la piscine.
- Avoid presenting a new word in its written form as pupils will attempt to pronounce the word according to its spelling – for example *comment* (comment t'appelles-tu?) becomes *comment* (do you have a comment to make?). Lots of pronunciation practice first, then show the written word. For the same reason, avoid putting unknown words up on display.
- Encourage pupils to listen and look for cognates – *mars* and *March*; *téléphone* and *telephone*; *Irlande* and *Ireland* etc..
- Split longer words and phrases into syllables – jan-vi-er, la-date-auj-ourd-hui-est.
- Begin to build up a good song collection – these are really useful ways of presenting and practising new language.

Practising language

Pupils will not learn any new language unless they are given lots of opportunity to practise it first – and some will need far more practice than others! You can provide additional practice by differentiating pair activities and general worksheets, limiting the amount of language required, or introducing carousel activities, where you can move around the class focusing a little more on individual progress and offering more personalized support. Group children of similar ability at the same table when you do this, as it makes the carousel easier to manage.

Practising language: key points

- Encourage 'full' sentences in response to questions, but don't expect them straightaway – one-word answers are often enough to indicate whether a child is beginning to understand – and motivate those of lesser ability to keep having a go, whereas the expectation of a full sentence might put them off.
- Use lots of question-and-answer activities to encourage the whole class to listen and speak (oui/non; vrai/faux; son/silence (sound and silence) pupils make an agreed sound if what you say is correct, and remain silent if it isn't, or the other way round!) – allow whole-group responses, but keep them on their toes by prompting for individual responses too.
- Rapid-fire questions around the whole class – either with the same question, or with a series of questions – you start by asking one pupil, who responds, then asks the next pupil the same question.
- Give choices in questions – tu préfères jouer au foot ou jouer au tennis?
- Give pupils lots of opportunity to ask questions, as well as answer them.
- Use all four skills to practise – not just speaking and listening.
- Don't feel obliged to correct every spoken error, but when you do, you can 'whisper' the correct response, repeat the phrase correctly without drawing attention to it, have a 'round-up' at the end of the lesson saying 'today, I heard a couple of things I'm not sure about' and either say or write the errors asking the whole group to identify what might be wrong.
- Use games to practise language – see Games Galore! for some games ideas.
- Keep revisiting language – games and quizzes are the best way of revisiting 'old' topics

Producing language

Practice activities work well for production too! Use classroom conversation, role-play, assemblies, displays, worksheets, information swap with partner school, and creative projects to embed language. 'Copying' is an initial element of production, but shouldn't be laboured over – get pupils used to recreating written French from memory. Avoid long swathes of text to copy, it's very boring! A small number of short, sharp phrases is enough to get the ball rolling. Don't ask pupils to copy from the board – having to lift your eyes from paper to board, then lower them down again, a number of times can be very off-putting for all pupils, and an additional hurdle for those who struggle a little with writing.

Working with the Key Stage 2 Framework for Languages

Don't be put off by the size of the KS2 Framework for Languages – this is a document absolutely overflowing with ideas for teaching activities, learning objectives and progression across the four year groups of KS2. If your school or institution doesn't already have a copy, you can download it at: **www.standards.dfes.gov.uk/primary/ publications/languages/framework/** but be warned – it's a huge document, and available for download only in individual parts, which makes downloading rather onerous. There's a link on the Standards website to the publications office if you need to order additional copies. Clips of teachers talking about how they use the Framework in planning are available on: **www.primarylanguages.org.uk/Teachers/ Using-the-KS2-Framework/**

The core strands:

- Oracy – listening, speaking, spoken interaction.
- Literacy – reading and writing.
- Intercultural understanding – develop greater understanding of their own lives, look at things from other perspectives, insight into people, culture and traditions of other countries.

The 'cross-cutting' strands:

- Knowledge about language (KAL) – develop insights into the nature of language and its social and cultural value, develop understanding of how language works.
- Language learning strategies (LLS) – develop strategies applicable to the learning of any language, including their own, develop awareness of their own preferred learning strategies.

If your language teaching programme doesn't yet start at Year 3, it's entirely appropriate to 'dip in and out' of the various objectives and outcomes to create a programme appropriate for your pupils. Use the framework to enable you to plan for mixed ability groupings, and to challenge children of all abilities – for example, Year 3 pupils may well be able to engage with longer texts, with some unknown words, inferring meaning from context, and using a bilingual dictionary to help them access a specific number of unknown words. Year 6 pupils will still enjoy a song or two – just remember to increase their repertoire gradually – the same old song over and over again ceases to be a learning or participatory activity, and becomes somewhat robotic!

Schemes of Work

There are a number of Schemes of Work on the market, many with supporting materials such as PowerPoints, CD-ROMS and worksheets. It can be difficult to know which one to buy, unless it's on personal recommendation, so if a publisher offers inspection copies, do request one, and take some time to decide whether it will suit your particular context. You might like to refer to the National Advisory Centre on Early Language Learning (NACELL) resources review page on: **www.nacell.org. uk/resources/teaching_materials.htm**

There's also a checklist of things to look for when deciding on what resources to buy. You may prefer to put together your own Scheme of Work for your particular class, and the Framework will provide you with guidelines and ideas. Alternatively, a simple Web search under 'KS2 languages Schemes of Work' will provide you with many examples of schemes posted on the Web by schools and local authorities. It's tempting to look at too many, so just choose a small number to browse and get ideas from.

You will find the QCA KS2 Languages Schemes of Work a very useful resource. These are fully available online at **www.qca.org.uk/qca_7055.aspx** and there is also a Teachers' Guide on this page. Current languages offered are French, German and Spanish, and they comprise 24 units to cover all four year groups at KS2.

Ideas for assessing progress in language learning

There are several ways you can monitor and capture progress effectively, and actively involve pupils in setting targets and understanding their achievements. There is no statutory requirement to assess progress in language learning at KS2, but there are non-statutory guidelines that you can use in conjunction with the Framework to help you plan and assess, and to help young learners understand where they are up to. The guidelines are linked to the KS3 languages guidelines and give information on:

- knowledge, skills and understanding
- links with other subject
- attainment targets (ATs)

The attainment targets relate to particular language skills:

- attainment target 1: listening and responding
- attainment target 2: speaking
- attainment target 3: reading and responding
- attainment target 4: writing

There are four levels to each AT, for example, AT2 (speaking):

- Level 1: Pupils respond briefly, with single words or short phrases, to what they see and hear. Their pronunciation may be approximate, and they may need considerable support from a spoken model and from visual clues.

- Level 4: Pupils take part in simple structured conversations of at least three or four exchanges, supported by visual or other cues. They are beginning to use their knowledge of grammar to adapt and substitute single words and phrases. Their pronunciation is generally accurate, and they show some consistency in their intonation.
- Now look at Level 5 to see how you might challenge more able pupils at KS2: Pupils take part in short conversations, seeking and conveying information and opinions in simple terms. They refer to recent experiences or future plans, as well as everyday activities and interests. Although there may be some mistakes, pupils make themselves understood with little or no difficulty.

The level descriptors are not qualitative in nature, that is, they do not tell you how well a pupil is able to do a particular activity, nor to what extent language is really embedded. You can add sub-levels to give both you and your pupils a qualitative insight, and to help you decide what to do to enhance learning.

Example:

Writing, Level 3

Pupils write two or three short sentences on familiar topics, using aids [for example, textbooks, wallcharts and their own written work]. They express personal responses [for example likes, dislikes and feelings]. They write short phrases from memory and their spelling is readily understandable.

Sub-levels:

1 I can do this by myself, with few or no errors.
2 I can do this with some help from my workbooks, with no errors, and would like some more practice to help me do it by myself.
3 I can do this when I look at my workbooks, or ask my teacher for help. I would like some more practice so that I can work towards doing it by myself.

In your sub-levels, try to avoid 'negative' language – 'I can't do that' can be demotivating – the idea is to work with pupils on understanding where they are, and what they feel they need to move on.

Encourage pupils to reword the levels for themselves – they can then stick them in their workbooks as a checklist to work through.

Example:

Listening and responding, Level 1
- I can understand single words, short phrases and some full sentences that my teacher uses.

Speaking, Level 1
- I can say single words and short phrases, even some full sentences. I need a bit of time to think of the right words, and my pronunciation sounds quite French!

Reading and responding, Level 1
- I can read single words, and some short sentences, and know what they mean. It helps when there are pictures to go with the words.

Writing, Level 1
- I can copy words and sentences we've done in class correctly. I've labelled items in French and created some French display work.

Remember, the levels don't correspond to a particular year group – pupils' progress and the levels they reach all depends on when they start to learn French, on how much French they actually do, and on their general cognitive and academic development and ability – so it may be that pupils both in Year 6 and in Year 3 reach Level 2 across the ATs by the end of the school year.

To view the full guidelines online, go to: www.nc.uk.net/nc_resources/html/MFL_k2.shtml or order a hard copy of the National Curriculum for Modern Foreign Languages from the link on the National Curriculum Online homepage http://www.nc.uk.net/ – the KS2 guidelines are towards the back of the curriculum document, though you will find the information on the KS3 curriculum and Programmes of Study of interest, and it's useful to understand the notion of progression across the Key Stages. If you have time, have a look at www.ncaction.org.uk/subjects/mfl/index.

htm – this gives a lot of useful information about both KS3 and 2 languages, covering topics such as assessment and progression in learning.

The European Languages Portfolio (ELP)

I'd heartily recommend you look at the ELP. Even if you decide not to follow it, it will certainly give you some good ideas on how to monitor and assess progress. The ELP is published by the National Centre for Languages (CILT), and fully available for download, along with a Teacher's Guide, at: **www.nacell.org.uk/resources/pub_ cilt/portfolio.htm**

The Languages Ladder

The Languages Ladder is a more formal way of assessing progress, and is a national recognition scheme for languages. It's suitable for all ages, in both formal and informal learning contexts, and captures achievement in speaking, listening, reading and writing across a number of levels of competence. Learners tend to progress at different rates in the four skills, and this method of assessment recognizes that. Remember though that some language learners need a blend of all four skills in their language programme to access new language successfully, even if their progress within individual skills is not uniform. It's administered by Asset Languages and I suggest you contact them directly for information about how to enter your pupils for examinations – **www. assetlanguages.co.uk** or **assetlanguages@ocr.org.uk**. The Languages Ladder is also a good way for teachers to 'test' themselves – so you may like to consider working your way up it too!

You can devise your own assessment sheets and activities too – have a look at some examples of these on: **www.nacell.org.uk/bestpractice/assrec.htm**

Brushing up rusty language skills

Most pre- and in-service primary teachers I've spoken to cite rusty language skills as a key barrier to their confidence in teaching French – but don't worry, you can brush up your skills in a number of ways, from enrolling in a night-school class (not always an option for busy teachers), private tuition (ditto!) to buying a language course, and working on your own. All of these have financial implications, but funding may be available through your local authority – ask the Modern Languages Advisor. If you choose a night-school programme, or a teach-yourself course, do think about your current skills, and think about what you most need to enable you to teach French effectively at KS2 – and look carefully at what's on offer – the courses may not provide what you most need.

Have a look at 'Teachers Talking French' on **www.ttfrench.com/** – this resource has been created entirely with primary teachers in mind. Use the KS2 and KS3 Modern Languages Schemes of Work (**www.standards.dfes.gov.uk/schemes2/secondary_mff/**) as a brush-up resource for yourself, and also look at what's on offer at the BBC Languages website, **www.bbc.co.uk/languages** – this also has a brief but useful skills audit.

Looking at the KS3 Schemes of Work (SoW) will also give you some idea of the kind of language and structures that pupils in Year 7 and beyond will cover. Use the vocabulary/phrase bank and the audio pronunciation guide with this book to brush up on your French accent and phrases – these can be accessed via **www. continuumbooks.com/resources/97808264988960**. Try a search under 'online French course' and have a browse – many are free! Here are a couple to get you started: **www. bonjourdefrance.com/** or **phonetique.free.fr**

If you're online and need particular words quickly, try **dictionnaire.tv5.org. dictionnaires.asp** or **www.wordreference.com/enfr/**. Keep up to date with current affairs with a quick daily glance at the **news.google.fr/** or **fr.news.yahoo.com/** or the homepage of any French search engine and click on 'Actualités' for a French perspective on events in the UK – even if your French is really rusty, set aside 20 minutes a week, choose an item that is of interest to you, and work through it, remembering to focus on what you do know, and rather than what you don't – inferring meaning from context is something you will be encouraging your pupils to do, and this is excellent practice. Alternatively, simply search for any topic that interests you, perhaps starting with your home town, and see what the French have to say about it, for example: **www.linternaute.com/voyage/royaume-uni/liverpool/**

You might like to explore the possibility of having a French Language Assistant in your school for a year. Take a look at **www.britishcouncil.org/languageassistants** – if you have a teacher training provider in your region, it's worth giving them a ring, as they often have overseas trainee teachers to place in a UK primary school for anything from two weeks to up to a year. An assistant is a fantastic resource for the whole school, staff and pupils alike, and can offer invaluable insight into language and culture.

2 Hello France!
Salut la France!

Looking at France

I've found that teaching a language to children works a lot better when they can contextualize its use *as* a language – as a real means of communication for many people. To do that, it helps if they can understand where the language is spoken, what the country looks like, where it is, how you get there, and so on. Making the language relevant is key to motivating pupils to learn it. Relating language and culture to pupils' own experiences, comparing and contrasting, exploring and understanding, are all effective ways of engaging pupils' interest, and moving learning beyond the level of simple games and basic language.

In my first few lessons with a new group of pupils I like to have a series of whole-group discussions about 'where we live' to act as a springboard for recognizing and understanding similarities and differences with the target country. A variation of this for older children is to stage small-group brainstorming activities, with one child from each group reporting back to the whole class. We also look at a map of the UK in relation to Europe, sometimes spending time first on looking at the UK itself, where we are (England, the North West, the North East etc.), what and where the other countries of the UK are, what and where the capital cities are, explaining to younger children what the function of a capital city is. This is a great way into talking about France and other countries where French is spoken (see 'French throughout the world – les pays francophones' for a more global picture of where French is spoken), and works equally well for promoting their understanding of their own environment.

Activity

A series of group introductory discussion topics may look like this:

- Where do we live?
- What languages are spoken in our community?

- What's our village/town/city like?
- What area of England do we live in?
- What's the capital of England, and where is it?
- What are England's most recognizable landmarks?
- What does UK stand for?
- What does GB stand for?
- What other countries form part of the UK/GB and what are their capital cities?

You could stage the discussion as follows:

- Note the group observations on the board, or nominate a pupil to do so.
- If you are working with small groups, give each group a piece of A3 paper and a marker pen. Each group must nominate a 'writer' who will write the group's observations on the A3, and a 'speaker', who will report back to the class using the sheet of A3 as a reference.
- Save the notes, either as a Word document or in bullet point form in PowerPoint, as you can use these later for comparison activities.
- As an extension activity, pupils can create visual displays based on the discussion, which can be complemented by displays about a particular area of France.

Depending on the Year Group, you can introduce the subject of France via a series of questions, or *un petit quiz* (oral or written) to establish what the pupils know about France already. Additionally, you can have *un petit quiz* after several lessons, which always works well, particularly if there is a prize involved! Some of the questions you might ask at the beginning are:

- What language(s) is/are spoken in France?
- What is the capital of France?
- What continent is France in?
- How far away is France from England?
- Do you know any kinds of French food?
- Do you know any famous landmarks or places?

Introducing France as a topic can follow the same sequence as above. I tend to introduce France in the context of Europe, and in relation to England as means of promoting pupils' more general geographical awareness.

Examples:

Display a map of Europe on the interactive whiteboard (IWB). If you don't have an IWB, simply stick a large paper map on the board at the front of the classroom. If you have a globe in the classroom, or can borrow one from a colleague, gather the pupils around it and point out where England is, and where mainland Europe is.

- Talk about how we might be able to travel to France – if any of your pupils have been to France, they will be keen to talk about it.
- Talk about what countries border France, and what languages are spoken there.
- Discuss the size of France in relation to other countries – is it bigger, smaller, or about the same size? Discuss population sizes.
- Point out Paris and other capital cities.
- Talk about the currency.

Activity

You can also ask pupils to find out a number of facts about France prior to the lesson. Make this homework appropriately challenging – Years 3 and 4 can happily find out at least 5 facts, Years 5 and 6 can easily cope with more. You might prefer to give some guidance about the kinds of information pupils can look for. Include any of the facts from the *petit quiz*, and other ones such as

- the longest river
- the biggest city
- the highest mountain
- the colours and name of the French flag
- the words for 'hello' and 'goodbye' in French
- a famous French writer
- a famous French composer
- a famous French artist
- a famous French sportsperson
- the name of the President
- other countries where French is spoken

Activity

Give the pupils an A4 exercise book purely for information and facts about France and the French language – depending on the kinds of things you are going to introduce into your language programme, call it 'All about France and the French', 'Salut la France!' or give it a more 'French' flavour – 'la France et les pays francophones'. You might choose something like 'la langue et la culture françaises' for older children. You can also divide the book into separate sections, each dealing with a specific topic, adding to the content throughout the year:

- La France: faits divers (some facts on France)
- Les pays francophones (other countries where French is spoken)
- L'Europe/la Communauté Européene (Europe and the European Community)
- Les religions (religions in France)
- Les jeunes gens (young people)
- Les grandes villes (French cities)
- Le transport (transport in France)
- L'éducation (education in France)
- Les français célèbres (famous French people)
- Le sport (sport, including Le Tour de France)

Use photographs, ClipArt, magazine pictures or other images to illustrate the book. Encourage pupils to collect images they think are relevant to the topic you are working on, and plan time in lessons to stick them into the exercise books. Over the course of a year, this builds into a piece of work pupils can feel really proud of.

You will find lots of interesting stuff on the French Embassy children's site (**www.ambafrance-uk.org/-Just-4-Kids-.html**). These pages are also available in French which is a great way for pupils and busy teachers to improve their French! Browse through it for classwork and homework ideas – the areas I've found most useful are:

- Fun facts – including 'do French people really eat frogs and snails?' – this is good to talk about cultural stereotypes.
- History, including an overview of the twentieth century and a look at contemporary France.
- Geography, including some information about *les pays francophones*.
- A look at France, with a short description of the lives of two French children.
- Sport, with information about famous French sportspeople.
- Arts and music with some lovely photographs of French cities and landmarks – all these pages have further links to relevant websites.

France at a glance: fast facts for the classroom

Geography – géographie

- The English Channel is called *la Manche* in French, and it's the shortest distance (about 26 miles) between England and France.
- France is bordered by eight countries – Andorra, Belgium, Germany, Italy, Luxembourg, Monaco, Spain and Switzerland.
- France is the biggest country in Western Europe.
- The most famous river is the Seine, which runs through Paris, with a small island called *Ile de Seine*.
- The longest river is the Loire, which runs through the beautiful Loire valley, also famous for its wine growing and *châteaux*.
- The highest mountain in France is called Mont Blanc – it's also the highest mountain in Europe! A tunnel runs through it, linking France to Italy.
- The Pyrénées mountains are in south-west France, and separate France and Spain.
- The hill range in central France is called le Massif Central.

- The Dordogne region (southwestern France) is home to the world-famous Lascaux Caves which boast 16,000 year-old cave paintings – and is also classed as a World Heritage Site. Take a virtual tour of the caves: **www.culture.gouv. fr/culture/arcnat/lascaux/en/** (there's also a link to the site in French!)

Festivals and other celebrations! – Fêtes!

- **French National Day, or Bastille Day** (la Fête Nationale française) was established in 1880, and is celebrated every year on 14 July. It's a really big celebration! This date marks the birth of the Republic, *la République Française*, and the end of the Monarchy in France. The Bastille was a notorious prison, hated and feared by the people of Paris, and considered a symbol of the corrupt governing system. It was stormed by revolutionaries on 14 July 1789, which sparked the French Revolution.
- **April Fool's Day** is a popular day for children – it's called *poisson d'avril* (April's fish) and pupils try to hang a paper fish on their teachers without their knowing!
- Many villages and small towns hold annual celebrations, often linked with religion or harvest time. A lot of people like to dress in traditional costume for these events.
- **Père Noël** brings small gifts on 6 December in many regions of France – this is the feast of St Nicholas.
- **Le réveillon de Noël**! (Christmas Eve!): Children leave their shoes by the fireplace for Père Noël to leave gifts in.
- Families decorate Christmas trees with tinsel, stars and lights a few days **before Christmas Day** – and when children awake on **Christmas morning** they often find things that *Père Noël* has left – nuts, fruits, sweets and little toys.
- Nativity scenes or cribs (crèches) are very popular in many French homes.
- **La bûche de Noël (Christmas log)** – a tasty treat! Have a go at baking one: **www.info-france-usa.org/kids/vocable/buche.htm**!

Landmarks, monuments and culture – repères, monuments et culture

- The statue displayed in the **Place de la République** in Paris, and in many town squares and official buildings throughout France, is called Marianne, and is a national emblem of France (ask pupils if the four countries of the UK have any national emblems!).

- **Notre Dame Cathedral** in Paris is over 800 years old!
- **The Arc de Triomphe** in Paris was built in 1836 as a celebration of Napoléon's victories. It sits in the centre of 12 avenues, including the very famous Champs Elysées.
- **The Mona Lisa** by Leonardo da Vinci, is housed in the Louvre, one of the biggest – and most famous – art galleries in the world, and is called *la Joconde* in French.

Daily life – la vie quotidienne

- It's common to kiss your friends once or even twice on alternate cheeks when you meet them.
- *La rentrée* (the return) is a big thing in France – it marks the start of the new school year and the end of the traditional summer break in July and August, so *au revoir les vacances*!

- In Paris, many people travel around by *métro*, short for *Métropolitain* – an underground railway like the Tube in London.
- You can travel around France at high speed on the TGV (train à grande vitesse).

Food and drink – nourriture et boissons

- These are very popular in France – and this is where we get the term *haute cuisine* from – this means 'fine food' but literally means 'high kitchen'. Even British restaurants can be awarded Michelin stars, which means they are extremely good restaurants, after the name of André Michelin, who wrote a very popular guide to France in 1900.
- It's estimated that there are over 300 different kinds of French cheeses – we get many of them here too, like Brie, Camembert and Port Salut.
- France is also famous for its wine – especially champagne, the fizzy wine from grapes grown in the Champagne area of France.
- We eat lots of French food too – baguettes, pains au chocolat, croissants, crêpes.

Lucky dip

- The Tour de France is an annual bike race, taking place every July – it's the world's biggest bike race, and goes on for over three weeks!
- There is no school uniform in France – ask pupils what they think about the benefits (or otherwise!) of wearing a school uniform, then get them to design their *uniforme idéal*!
- Eurodisney (**corporate.disneylandparis.fr/index.xhtml**), a huge Disney theme park to the east of Paris – you can travel directly to it on the métro! There's another famous park too – *Parc Astérix*, all about Astérix the Gaul and his friends! (**www.parcasterix.fr/**)

Take a trip round the culture of France on: **www.discoverfrance.net/**

Famous France: Some fast facts on les français célèbres and ideas for cross-curricular links

Activity

Exploring famous French or French-speaking people makes for an interesting topic over a series of lessons, for individual project work, as well as for introducing pupils to, and engaging them with, discussion about other topics and issues. Start off by drawing up a list of famous British people – give some 'easy' categories like 'famous British footballers' or 'famous British singers' to get the ball rolling, then introduce some more challenging ones, like 'famous British explorers' or 'famous British scientists' – get them on the trail of Alan Turing for example. I've given four people per category, though there are many more people – and categories!

Historical figures – personnages historiques

- **Guillaume le Conquérant (1027–87)** – William the Conquerer – he's French! Link with King Harold, 1066 and the Battle of Hastings, and take a look at Normandy.
- **Napoléon Bonaparte (1769–1821)** – the first Emperor of France and a very famous French general – look at the French Revolution, the Arc de Triomphe, and Corsica (la Corse) – you'll find some lovely clips on YouTube!
- **Gustave Eiffel (1832–1923)** – architect who designed and built the Eiffel Tower in 1889 – look at famous structures in the UK, and talk about who designed and built them – try Sir Christopher Wren, Isambard Kingdom Brunel and Anthony Gormley.
- **King Louis XIV (1638–1715)** – look at his grandson, Louis XVI, who was the last King of France, the Palace of Versailles, and the role of monarchy – discuss what other European countries still have a monarchy.

Literature – la littérature

- **Jean de la Fontaine (1621–95)** – an absolute must for the primary school! Writer of famous fables (this is where we get the word 'fabulous' from) such as 'The Crow and the Fox' and 'The Hare and the Tortoise' – explore Aesop too –

La Fontaine got a lot of his ideas from him! Talk about the nature of fables, and compare that to other forms of storytelling or writing, like fairy tales, poetry (rhyming and non-rhyming, and what works best), novels, short stories, plays.

- **Charles Perrault (1628–1703)** – another absolute must for the primary school! Generally credited with creating the fairy tale, he wrote amongst other things 'Le petit chaperon rouge' ('Little Red Riding Hood'), 'Cendrillon' ('Cinderella') and 'La Belle au bois dormant' ('Sleeping Beauty') – look at his work in both French and English, talk about the nature of the fairy tale, and take a look at the Brothers Grimm too. Roald Dahl wrote some rather subversive (but funny!) versions of fairy tales – *Revolting Rhymes* – use extracts from them to compare language and prose, and to discuss how writers might choose certain words to tell the same story but in a different way.

- **Victor Hugo (1802–85)** – not only a poet and writer, but a human rights activist too (a bit like Dickens!). Look at *Notre Dame de Paris* (*The Hunchback of Notre Dame*) and the notion of film adaptations and judging people by how they look – similarly with *Les Misérables* – talk about musical theatre, and what brought about the French Revolution.

- **Georges Rémi (1907–83)** – the Belgian cartoonist and writer otherwise known as 'Hergé' (a play on the sound his initials make!), famous for *Les Aventures de Tintin* – this is a fantastic introduction to the art of writing comic books – explore some of Tintin's adventures with your pupils, and create some storyboards or comic strips of your own, coming up with new characters, and working out how to tell a story through direct speech, with only minimal side comments – use the speech bubbles facility in Word to create some simple stories first.

If time is pressing, take a shortcut to literature, writers, poets and playwrights in both French and English: **fr.wikisource.org/wiki/Accueil** or **en.wikisource.org/wiki/Main_Page**

Art – l'art

- **Auguste Renoir (1841–1919)** – a famous Impressionist, some of his best-known works include *La Balançoire* (*The Swing*) and *Bal au moulin de la Galette* (*Ball at the Galette Windmill*).
- **Henri Cartier-Bresson (1908–2004)** – a photographer whose images of everyday life in Paris – 'street photography' became world-famous.

- **Toulouse Lautrec (1864–1901)** – a post-Impressionist artist, his work included not only paintings, but also posters, many used to advertise shows at the famous Moulin Rouge.
- **René Magritte (1898–1967)** – a Belgian artist in the school of Surrealism – try *La Trahison des images*, better known as *Ceci n'est pas une pipe* or *This is not a pipe* – which it clearly is – but it is only an *image* of a pipe! Exercise a little caution with Magritte's images – some are unsuitable for primary-age children.

For a wonderful online browse around art galleries, have a look at: **www.artcyclopedia. com/**

 Teaching tip

Download an image by a French artist, sculptor or photographer. Discuss the image in English, describe it, talk about why they think it's 'good' or 'bad', and then see if pupils can recreate it.

Science – la science

- **René Descartes (1596–1650)** – scientist, mathematician and philosopher – creator of the famous 'cogito ergo sum' – je pense donc je suis – I think therefore I am – have some fun with this when discussing hobbies – I've had great responses from pupils: Je joue au foot donc je suis; Je danse donc je suis!
- **Marie Curie (1867–1934)** – look at Poland, Warsaw, radioactivity, nuclear power, X-rays, the dangers of sun-bathing, Nobel Prize.
- **Pierre Curie (1859–1906)** – born in Paris, worked with his wife on radioactivity.
- **Louis Pasteur (1822–95)** – look at bacteria, disease, vaccination, immune system, and link with Edward Jenner, Joseph Lister and Alexander Fleming. We get the term 'pasteurization' from his name!

Other categories can include:

Classical music; modern music; sport; film; inventions; architecture. Remember all the categories work particularly well when looked at together with famous English-speaking people from the same ones!

A European perspective: countries and capitals of Europe – pays et capitales d'Europe

A good way of introducing Europe as a topic, or reinforcing pupils' knowledge about Europe, is to teach a number of countries and their capitals in French. It also offers a great opportunity to practise all four skills. The number of countries and capitals you introduce depends on the year group – for example, between 6 and 10 might be a good number for Year 3, whereas Year 6 can face the challenge of 20 plus over a couple of lessons.

Activity

The following sequence works well, though you can leave various steps out according to your pupils' prior knowledge, or according to your own preference:

- Choose the countries you will focus on.
- In English, ask the whole group to name as many countries in Europe as they can (some pupils may need reminding that England, Scotland, Wales, Northern and Southern Ireland are also a part of Europe).
- Note these on the board, prompting pupils to include your own chosen countries if they do not mention them.
- Highlight the countries you have decided to focus on.
- Ask the pupils what the capital cities are, and note these on the board also. You can proceed with the French words even if the pupils cannot remember the capital cities exactly – you will reinforce this knowledge using French.
  Introduce the question:

Quelle est la capitale	de	l'Angleterre?
	de	l'Écosse?
	du	pays de Galles?
	de	la France?

You may want to prompt whole-sentence responses such as: la capitale de la France est Paris. Younger or less able children may respond better if they are allowed to give single-word responses.

Phrase your questions or statements differently to keep the pace up:

> *Oui/non* (yes/no) questions: Est-ce que Madrid est la capitale de l'Allemagne?
>
> *Vrai/faux* (true/false) statements: Edimbourg est la capitale de l'Écosse – where it's 'faux', prompt the pupils for the correct response.

Activity

If you want to work more with the written word, write out each country and capital in French on a separate piece of card. Stick the country cards on the board, and ask pupils to choose the correct capital to stick beneath it. If you have time, stick the country cards up with the capital cards below, some in the right place, some not. Pupils have to say which cards are in the right place, and adjust the others accordingly. Go to **www.continuumbooks.com/resources/97808264988960** to download and print out some country and capital card sheets to start you off: **Worksheet 1: Country and Capital Cards**. You might decide to enlarge to A3 using a photocopier to ensure that the words are big enough for pupils to see. Alternatively, make 'snap' cards out of them – photocopy onto A4 card several times, then cut out the individual squares to create a number of 'snap' packs. With the same cards, play 'Où es-tu?' – one group of pupils gets a 'country' card each, whilst the second group gets a 'capital' card. Walking round the classroom, they have to find their partner – Où es-tu? Je suis en France! – if the person asking the question is in Paris (Je suis à Paris), they've found their partner! If not, both carry on searching!

Activity

As an additional literacy activity in keeping with the Framework, encourage pupils to compare both the 'look' (the written word) and the 'sound' (the spoken word) of the countries and capitals in English and French.

If you are focusing on listening skills, before you introduce the new words formally, say them quite slowly, asking pupils to guess the English equivalent of the French word (Londres and London shouldn't prove too much of a challenge!).

Activity

It won't take long to prepare a worksheet or a quiz about capitals. Pupils can also label maps of Europe in English or in French (remember to include a word reference bank). You could provide a map with the names of the countries and capitals given in English, and pupils choose from the French reference bank – or vice versa.

Go to www.continuumbooks.com/resources/97808264988960 to download and print out **Worksheet 2: Les capitales!** which will encourage pupils to focus both on their knowledge of Europe, and on their French spelling. The instructions are given bilingually – but do avoid always giving instructions in both languages, it can make pupils rather lazy! Remember it's always a good idea to give an additional creative or 'thinking' task as an extension activity for those pupils who finish very quickly. To encourage less able pupils to engage more in similar tasks, reduce the number of questions that you give them to enable them to work through the worksheet at a slightly increased pace.

Activity

Prepare a gap exercise: for example: Paris est la capitale de la _____. You can make this a 'double-gap' exercise to encourage pupils to look very carefully at individual words, and to work on spelling, for example: B_er_ _ n est la capitale de

Grammar point

De changes according to the gender or spelling of the particular country you're talking about. When a country is feminine, as in *la France*, add the word *la* to get: Quelle est la capitale de la France? Where the country begins with a vowel, *de* becomes *de l'*, as in: Quelle est la capitale de l'Écosse?. If the country is masculine, such as *le Portugal* then *de* changes to *du* and the question becomes: Quelle est la capitale du Portugal? Where the country is in the plural, *de* becomes *des*.

Use the following as an aide-mémoire for both you and the pupils:

- de + la = de la – la capitale **de la France** est Paris.
- de + le = du – la capitale **du Portugal** est Lisbonne.
- de + les = des – la capitale **des Pays Bas** est Amsterdam
- de + l' = de l' – la capitale **de l'Italie** est Rome.

If you're keen to practise this grammar point, write a series of sentences either on the board or on a worksheet with some errors in it:

For example:

- Où sont les erreurs? Soulignez!
- Berne est la capitale du Suisse
- Bruxelles est la capitale de la Belgique
- Londres est la capitale des l'Angleterre

Pupils have to look for the errors and underline them. Prompt them for the correct response. This kind of activity also reinforces the notion of gender, singular and plural.

European flags – les drapeaux européens

I use flags both as a means of visually reinforcing countries and capitals, as a means of promoting general knowledge and to introduce colours. I start by looking at the Union Jack, and the individual flags of England, Scotland, Wales and Northern Ireland. I often use the French flag to decorate worksheets and visual displays. Try **world-flags.info/Europe/europe.html** or **en.wikipedia.org/wiki/Flags_of_Europe** for a comprehensive list of European countries and their flags.

Activity

Go to **www.continuumbooks.com/resources/97808264988960** to download and print out **Worksheet 3: Flag flashcards.** (If you have a whiteboard, use the PowerPoint presentation as this can be less time-consuming. The presentation allows you to show the flag first, then the name of the country in writing after the pupils have said it. Choose the number of flags you want to focus on, holding up the flashcard, or screening the slides one by one. As you show the flag, ask 'c'est quel pays?' – pupils might know! If they don't, simply say the name the country or a full sentence, 'c'est le drapeau de la Suisse' for example. To practise the flags, use the *oui/non* or *vrai/faux* techniques.

Reinforcement activities include:

A worksheet for class time or homework, giving a series of flags asking pupils to identify the country (download **Worksheet 4: Les drapeaux**).

Download **Worksheet 5: Les couleurs des drapeaux** which shows a series of blank flags, giving a name of a country next to each one. Pupils have to fill in the correct colours.

Download **Worksheet 6: Match the flag** which presents two columns, one with a list of countries, the second with a series of flags out of sequence. Pupils have to match the countries to the flags by drawing a connecting line. Do this as a whole group activity by numbering the countries, and giving the flags a letter – pupils have to give the correct number/letter combination.

- Countries and capitals are a good topic for close comparison of written and spoken English and French – e.g. Lisbonne and Lisbon, Londres and London, Paris and Paris!

Use flags to introduce or practise colours. Download **Worksheet 7: Les couleurs des drapeaux** which shows blank flags with colours in French next to these. Pupils colour in the flags and name the countries.

- Write down the colours of a series of flags – pupils have to guess the flags from the colours.

> ### Information point
>
> The French flag is called *le Tricolore* referring to the three bands of colour –
> red, white and blue. You'll see the *Tricolore* displayed on all public buildings
> in France, such as the town hall – *l'hôtel de ville* or *la mairie*. A simple Web
> search combining the terms *le Tricolore* and *hôtel de ville*, even adding the
> name of a large town or city, will give you some fantastic images for display
> or teaching materials

There are some nice interactive sites for children to test their general knowledge of Europe – try **www.bfs.admin.ch/bfs/portal/fr/index/dienstleistungen/forumkids/ pays_d_europe.html** or **www.playkidsgames.com/problem_solveGames.htm** – have a good browse round this one, there are lots of fun problem-solving and fact-checking games. **simple.wikipedia.org/wiki/Europe** is a good site for pupils to pick up some basic – but key – information about Europe. **schools-wikipedia.org/wp/l/List_of_ European_countries.htm** – a nice shortcut!

Countries of the European Union (EU) – les pays de la Communauté Européene (EU)

Exploring the European Union makes for a really engaging research topic, which can start in Year 3, and be worked on over the whole of KS2. By the end of Year 6, pupils will have compiled an impressive dossier on the EU. Currently, there are 27 member states, and two candidate states.

Researching facts and compiling a dossier

Activity

Start pupils off with a simple research question such as 'What is the European Union?' This works well as an initial activity to get the ball rolling, and is particularly effective as a homework or small-group activity. To start them off, or for a quick brush-up on your own knowledge, consult the information bank below, or try the following website: **www.eurunion.org/infores/teaching/Young/fun.htm** This site offers a wealth of information and resources designed for children, and includes:

- an audiovisual library with copyright-free photographs, ClipArt, video and audio files, with an additional 'multimedia' link; comics, and brochures about Europe, with an information email address – this makes for an excellent activity in itself – in pairs or small groups, pupils draw up a list of questions about the EU. As a whole group, decide on a manageable number of questions on a range of topics, and during an IT lesson, each pupil sends a particular question or series of questions, collating the responses as they arrive for eventual presentation to the whole class – there is also a dedicated 'Eurodesk' you can contact via email.
- 'Environment for young Europeans' – a useful cache of information if you want to make the environment a topic to focus on.
- 'EU minichefs' – food always goes down well!
- 'Euromyths' and 'Get your facts straight' – some very odd stories about the EU – work out what's true and what's not!
- 'EuropaGO' – games and other fun activities.
- 'Youth forum' – a great forum for young people to swap ideas and information with direct links to the websites of member states' embassies – many with dedicated children's areas.

encarta.msn.com/encyclopedia_761579567/European_Union.html
uk.encarta.msn.com/encyclopedia_761579567/European_Union.html
These sites have useful maps and other images.
simple.wikipedia.org/wiki/European_Union
The language on the simple wikipedia pages are not as complex as the 'main' wikipedia pages. **en.wikipedia.org/wiki/European_Union**
Children may find the language somewhat dense on the wikipedia pages, but they can be appropriate for children of high ability – and also for picking out key facts yourself. **schools-wikipedia.org/wp/l/List_of_European_Union_member_states_by_accession.htm**
www.europe.org.uk/index/-/id/259/
This is a simple but comprehensive round-up of facts about Europe.
Facts to gather can include:

- current member states
- current candidate states

- flag – it's blue, with 12 gold stars, representing ideals of perfection and unity

- official language/s
- how to say 'hello' and 'goodbye' in the official language/s
- capital city
- population
- currency
- date of joining the EU
- voting age
- name of President/Prime Minister
- bordering countries

You could also include:

- One key fact about the country to be presented in the form of 'fast facts' or *le saviez-vous? le savais-tu?* ('did you know . . . ?') which could include sporting triumphs, famous landmarks, food and drink and so on.
- One key visual image that pupils feel represents the country – get them to explain why they've chosen this particular one.

Be specific about the language pupils are to collect information in – for example, you may prefer to allow them to research and present facts in English, which supports a number of the 12 literacy strands of the Primary National Strategy. Additional language-specific activities might include finding out the names of the countries and capitals in French (use either a good bilingual dictionary, linking to general dictionary skill work, or try the WordReference online dictionary at: **www.wordreference.com/ fren/**); presenting key facts under specific headings in French, such as Pays, Capitale, Langue/s Officielle/s.

Activity

Once pupils have started gathering facts, they can type them into a Word table, with small grids. Print them out, then cut and glue onto cards to create a European Union general knowledge quiz. Colour-code the cards for topics, such as green for geographical or environmental facts, blue for capitals, red for currency and so on. Save the cards, and use them at the 'French Day'! Particularly popular questions that can stump adults (always a winner with children!) are capitals, currency and the colours of flags. A bonus prize for the person who can name all 27 member states!

Fast facts:

- The EU was founded in 1957, with an original membership of six countries.
- The original six countries were: France, Belgium, Luxembourg, West Germany, Holland (Netherlands) and Italy.
- The United Kingdom joined in 1973.
- When Germany reunited in 1990, the former East Germany was accepted into the EU.
- The Euro was introduced in 2002 (but the UK opted out, as did Denmark and Sweden!).
- The European Anthem is 'Ode to Joy', from Beethoven's Ninth Symphony.
- The motto of the EU is 'United in Diversity'.
- The EU is founded on four principles: peace, democracy, tolerance and equality.
- 9 May is Europe Day, commemorating 9 May 1950, when Robert Schuman, a French minister, presented his ideas for a unified Europe.

Looking at other languages

Activity

You might like to introduce your pupils to the 'look' of languages other than English and French. They can create a display of languages spoken throughout the EU, with the country and capital names, and the word for 'Hello' for example, in the language/s of those countries.

Try these to start you off:

- Austria – Österreich – Wien – Hallo!
- Czech Republic – Česká Republika – Praha – Ahoj!

- Finland – Suomi – Helsingfors – Hei!
- Germany – Deutschland – Berlin – Hallo!
- Ireland – Éire – Baile Átha Cliath – Dia Dhuit!
- Latvia – Latvija – Riga – Sveiki!
- Poland – Polska – Warszawa – Czeŝĉ!
- Spain – España – Madrid – ¡Hola!

For a full list, download Worksheet 8: Looking at other languages.

Information point

An internet search will lead you to audio files to check the pronunciation.

If you have any pupils who are bilingual or who speak English as an additional language (EAL pupils) in your class, ask them to add the details of their native country to the list – if you've carried out a school-wide survey of languages spoken in the school, add those too – this will build into a very impressive display.

European Day of Languages! (EDL) – Journée européene des langues

There's an annual celebration of language and culture on 26 September, where teachers and other people involved in language teaching and learning put on activities and events, many sharing their ideas via the CILT website (**www.cilt.org.uk**). In the run-up to September, try to visit the CILT website as often as you can for information, as well as free (and otherwise!) resources that you can send off for via CILT. You can also access information about events in previous years.

Understanding euros

Looking at currency is a good way of integrating numeracy, general knowledge about the wider European Community and a broader understanding of the value of money. A number of EU countries adopted the euro, introducing it as legal tender on 1 January 2002 (see the list of EU countries for details). Although the available coins and notes are the same in each of these countries, there is an important difference – the heads side of each coin (le côté face) is an image representing a significant person or symbol of that particular country. So for example, in Monaco, the coin has the face of Prince Rainier, in Ireland it has a Celtic harp and in Spain the coin shows a portrait of King Juan Carlos the First.

This 'fast fact' makes for a great *le saviez-vous/le savais-tu?* ('did you know . . . ?') fact.

Coins and notes – pièces et billets

Each euro is made up of one hundred cents.
Coins come in 1c, 2c, 5c, 10c, 20c, 50, 1€, 2€
Notes come in 5€, 10€, 20€, 50€, 100€, 200€, 500€.

Generally a euro is worth about 75p, though this can obviously fluctuate daily, sometimes quite dramatically, which makes for an interesting discussion in itself. For numeracy games, and looking at what things cost, I tend to stick at 75p, unless we are particularly looking up the daily exchange rate for comparative purposes (e.g. **www. reuters.co.uk** or **www.theonlineconverter.co.uk/conversions/currency.htm**).

Activity

Comparing prices of goods, particularly computer games and consoles, clothes and food items, in different countries, makes for a fascinating activity that pupils approach with gusto. You can extend that activity by comparing euro prices across

Europe – pupils can compare the price of a Manchester United team strip (maillot) in England (e.g. **manchesterunited.shopperuk.com/**), in France (e.g. **www.footcenter. fr/fr/football/boutique-e-manchester-united-man.html@adwor**) and in Belgium (e.g. **shopping-fr.kelkoo.be/ss-manchester-united-maillot.html**).

You can access lots of pictures of euros on the Web – I've used the following: **www. usmint.gov/KIDS/coinnews/theEuro.cfm**, **simple.wikipedia.org/wiki/Euro** (which also has a lovely image of the euro sign, and concise information on the euro itself) and **en.wikipedia.org/wiki/Image:Euro_banknotes.png** (as you'll see, this is a copyrighted image, so be careful about using the image on your your own material); **ec.europa. eu/euro/entry.html** and **www.deljpn.ec.europa.eu/union/showpage_en_union.emu. php** – scroll down the page for the pictures of euro banknotes and coins – there's also a link to another site with more pictures.

Activity

Create some numeracy puzzles using euros and pound sterling – give a series of prices in euros or in pound sterling, pupils have to convert each sum to the other currency.

Give your pupils a shopping list, and a certain amount of money, and send them shopping on:

- www.laredoute.fr/
- www.lebonmarche.fr/
- www.printemps.com/
- www.galerieslafayette.com/
- www.carrefour.fr/ – the Carrefour site is excellent for food shopping! You don't have to register, simply click on 'vos courses sur internet' which takes you to www.oopshop.com – now click on 'accès au rayons' (go to shelves) and browse every kind of product you can imagine!

Teaching tip

After you've been food shopping, make crêpes, with citron (lemon) – or chocolat – in fact, with anything the pupils like – get them to suggest ingredients, and talk about what's most healthy – then simply enjoy!

Make a healthy-eating calendar that pupils fill out for one full week – but do it in French! Use **Worksheet 9: Mon calendrier d'alimentation saine** as a template. Use the days of the week, the mealtimes (petit déjeuner, déjeuner, etc.), and the food and drink you've already covered – you can either have a huge one in class that has everyone's name on it, or create an A4 calendar for them to fill out at home and in school. If pupils don't know the right words, they can use an online dictionary in class. At the end of the week (or month!), draw up a list of Top Five healthy foods and drinks, and Top Five unhealthy ones – not necessarily the same as the favourite ones! A sticker for those who have managed 5 portions of fruit and vegetables a day – je mange mes cinq portions par jour – and perhaps a chocolate as a special treat! I've found it's a good idea to write a letter to parents explaining what you are doing – occasionally a parent may feel a little sensitive about diet and nutrition in general! Do let pupils write at least some of the calendar in English – particularly *mon objectif* and *commentaires* – where they reflect on whether they've achieved their objective, and what the goal for the following week might be! Parents can also include a comment in the comment box – you will get some very interesting ones!

French throughout the world – les pays francophones

Pupils are often astounded by how widely French is spoken throughout the world. Looking at French-speaking regions helps pupils understand how people have moved and migrated around the globe, taking their language and culture with them, and how new communities, new cultures and new ways of using language are born. Looking at world maps also enhances pupils' general understanding of where continents and countries are, and reinforces their geographical understanding. A quick search on any of the main search engine image pages will give you a huge number of maps highlighting *les pays francophones* – some are not suitable to screen on an IWB or to download into a worksheet (if copyright free) as the text is not particularly legible, so you may have to browse somewhat first till you find a suitable one for your purposes.

Activity

Show pupils the world map, with French-speaking countries highlighted. Discuss where these countries are. Ask pupils what they already know about them. Choose an appropriate number of countries per year group, and either as a homework or a small-group activity in the IT suite, ask pupils to gather at least five key facts about those countries. If you are considering setting up a school link with a French school, you may like to investigate the possibility of communicating with one farther afield! Life really can be enormously different in countries such as Mauritius or Haiti, and exploring those differences, and discovering similarities opens up a whole new vista of world view for pupils – and a package arriving from Mauritius or Haiti would indeed be a special treat!

Activity

A longer-term activity that pupils find interesting is a survey of the most widely spoken languages in the world – they often gasp in astonishment that Chinese is at the very top of the list. You may prefer to create a more structured survey for younger pupils, by giving them a list of countries/languages across the globe, and asking them to find out how many people speak those languages. Use **Worksheet 10: Languages of the World** as a starting point – it works well as homework, as pair work in the school library or as independent work in the IT suite. Do be careful though of solely Web-based research – a trawl through a number of reputable sites told me that there were 350 million French speakers, 700 million and so on – I verified the latest report from the French Embassy citing 200 million! (This is including native speakers, those who speak French as a second language, and those who are learning French: **www. ambafrance-uk.org/200-million-French-speakers-in-the.html**).

Encourage pupils to name the source they have got the information from – this is an important research skill and gives them a chance to practise! As a whole group, go through the responses, then discuss where the languages are most widely spoken. As a secondary ICT activity, when pupils have gathered the information, get them to design a table and put the languages in order of number of speakers – good for both design and numeracy skills!

You will find **www.nvtc.gov/lotw/** a very useful site both for yourself, and older pupils – younger pupils may find the language a little complex. Browse around the site – it's full of interesting facts with a handy summary of languages at **www.nvtc. gov/lotw/months/november/worldlanguages.htm**. Wikipedia also gives a concise summary:

en.wikipedia.org/wiki/List_of_languages_by_number_of_native_speakers

On parle français ici . . .

- Algeria
- Andorra
- Aosta Valley (Italy)
- Belgium
- Benin
- Burkina Faso
- Burundi
- Cameroon
- Canada (e.g. Montréal, Québec)
- Central African Republic
- Chad
- Comoros
- Democratic Republic of the Congo
- Dijbouti
- Equatorial Guinea
- France
- French Guyana
- Gabon
- Guadeloupe
- Guernsey (Channel Island)
- Guinea

- Haiti
- Côte d'Ivoire (Ivory Coast)
- Jersey (Channel Island)
- Lebanon
- Louisiana (USA)
- Luxembourg
- Madagascar
- Mali
- Martinique
- Mauritania
- Mauritius
- Monaco
- Morocco
- Niger
- Rwanda
- Sénégal
- Seychelles
- Switzerland
- Togo
- Tunisia
- Vanuatu
- Vatican State

Activity

Have a *Les langues – où dans le monde?* ('languages – where in the world?') research competition – pupils have a half-term to find out which continent each of these countries or regions are on, and/or which countries may border them, what other languages are spoken there and so on.

If you'd like more information about French-speaking countries, have a look at the official *la Francophonie* website – **www.francophonie.org/**.

Teaching tip

Always devote at least a small part of the lesson to the language itself – pupils need lots of exposure to language, and opportunities to practise and to reinforce it. These opportunities do arise during the school day, though at particular times of the year you may find it more challenging to exploit those opportunities, so do make sure that, if for example you've planned a unit of work focusing more on cultural and geographical awareness and understanding, you've allotted some time to language teaching and learning as well. Use starter games to keep up work on numbers and spelling, or teach, then practise, new vocabulary based on the topic, such as European countries and capitals in French.

Making friends in France and other French-speaking countries: creating school partnerships

Creating a partnership with schools in France or other French-speaking countries gives pupils an opportunity to use their French 'for real', giving them a sense of relevance and authentic purpose to language learning. It allows them to make friends with children of other countries and cultures, sharing experiences and broadening their outlook about life both at home and across the globe. For teachers too, it's a great way of learning about teachers' professional lives in the target country, and of sharing tips and strategies for teaching languages. Neither you nor your pupils have to have much target language to establish a successful partnership – pupils can be encouraged to write very clearly and neatly in their own language first – they will get lots of practice with French when reading the emails, letters and other communications from their partner pupils. If your school has access to email or video conferencing facilities, you can integrate ICT into the partnership work, but don't worry if it doesn't – it can work just as well the old-fashioned way – and the thrill of a parcel arriving from France is enormous!

The aims of the partnership

Before you start, I'd advise you think about what exactly it is you want to achieve by having a link with a French school, the kinds of information you'd like to swap, and the amount of time you and your pupils can realistically give to activities related to the partnership. To make the partnership successful, you and your partner teacher should ideally share the same aims for it. Your aims might include:

- give pupils an opportunity to practise their increasing language skills with native speakers

- enhance reading and writing skills
- enhance speaking and listening skills
- promote ICT skills
- enhance general communication and presentation skills
- increase understanding of social, religious and cultural life in the home and target country
- broaden pupils' horizons
- make friends!

Create a wish list of activities you'd like your pupils to engage in that you can discuss with your partner teacher – this will also help you plan your lessons around the partnership activities, ensuring that there is enough time for the pupils to actually create the resources and other materials you will exchange. Your wish list might include:

- descriptions of self and family, with photograph
- descriptions of home town, and school
- the school day
- favourite subjects at school, including reasons why
- school holidays – when, how long, and what there is to do during them!
- hobbies
- favourite sportspeople, singers or actors
- posters/collages about life in England, including topics such as food, public transport, festivals
- major cities and towns in the UK

It might also include:

- What jobs pupils would like to do when they leave school, and why – we know they'll probably change their minds many times before they do leave school, but getting them to think, talk and write about it encourages pupils to think about the opportunities open to them, and yields fascinating insights into how they view the world.

Talk to your pupils about it – canvass their opinions of what the potential benefits of linking with a French school might be, and what kinds of information they would like to share with their partner pupils. With your pupils, prepare an 'info pack' about your school for your partner institution, which can be presented either online or sent via post in hard copy – or both! Several months into the partnership, ask pupils to prepare a presentation or display about its benefits for the rest of the school. Invite the local press too!

Setting up the partnership

It's useful to have an idea of where geographically you'd best like your partnership school to be located, and what kind of school you'd like to work with . . . For example, would you prefer a large inner-city school or a small rural school? While the distinction sounds somewhat simplistic, balancing the importance of broadening your pupils' understanding of the world with the practicalities of common or likely interests, particularly if you are planning an exchange visit in the longer term, is something you may wish to consider.

To get help in finding a partnership school, you can contact:

- The languages department of your local secondary school or Specialist Languages College – they may well have established links with French or French-speaking secondary schools who can liaise with their own local primaries to find interested schools.
- The Modern Languages Coordinator or Adviser at your local authority.
- Send parents/carers/governors a letter asking if they have any useful contacts in the target country.
- Subscribe to one or more of CILT's email discussion lists, such as the Early Language Learning (ELL) forum, and ask colleagues on the list if they have any useful contacts or tips (**www.cilt.org.uk/keepintouch/index.htm** – scroll down to 'discussion lists' and click on the list you wish to join, then click on 'join or leave the list' – remember you can join as many or as few lists as you like!).
- You might also like to try *The Times Education Supplement* (*TES*) online 'Staffroom' – a good way of networking and sharing ideas – **www.tes.co.uk/ section/staffroom/**.
- **www.nacell.org.uk/networking/schools_links.htm** – this page offers a comprehensive list of websites you will find useful – for example there's a direct link to the British Council School Partnerships site – you'll have to browse around a little here to find the kind of information you might need – look for 'find a partnership school' (**www.britishcouncil.org/learning-ie-school-partnerships.htm**); you can also access the Global Gateway directly from here – another British Council site including a database on potential

partnership partners and other information on international projects, **www. globalgateway.org.uk/**.

- The *Association européene des enseignants* is well worth a look too, (**www. aede.org/**), and has a French version **www.aede-france.org/** which is useful for language practice. Look at the 'partner-finding' service on **www. elanguages.org/** – funded by the Department for Children, Families and Schools (DCFS) – a great site to browse and to find teachers and schools for collaborative language learning projects.
- **www.etwinning.net** – focusing on European partnerships linking via ICT.
- **www.epals.com/**.

A few points to remember:

- To support learning effectively, the most successful partnerships will require time and ongoing commitment – don't be disappointed if you are unable to find similar enthusiasm straightaway.
- Successful partnerships support learning and engagement in learning across the curriculum, not just in French.
- When you get a school contact name, don't be afraid to communicate with your contact partner in English if your French is a bit wobbly, just tell them that it *is* a little wobbly – they will understand that enhancing your own language skills plays an important role in the decision to establish a partnership in the first place.
- If you think your pupils will engage more effectively with the partnership by working in English in the first instance, agree that with your partner – they will be exposed to plenty of French language and culture when they read the communications from their partner pupils.
- Don't be put off by the thought of having to translate lots of French for your pupils – make this an integral part of lessons, using either a good online or hard-copy bilingual dictionary – remember that colleagues in your local secondary schools will be able to help with more complex language.
- If both you and your contact partner have access to broadband at school, think about meeting via desktop videoconferencing (such as Skype, **www. skype.com**) to get to know each other – this will work well for pupils too, when they have mastered some basic French, though you may need to 'direct' conversations at first, by suggesting some topics for discussion.
- You might like to try out a partnership with a UK-based school too – pupils may have similar baseline language skills, so you can insist on the use of French!

For an interesting 'info-swap', choose a school in an entirely different part of the UK from where you are based – a useful shortcut to finding a school is via the Education section of the BBC news website – **news.bbc.co.uk/** – this has a search facility by town name, so you can choose an area you find interesting, and look for the schools in that area – although the focus here is on league tables, I'm not promoting those as a criteria for partnership – just the search facility which will give you the contact details of primary schools you can approach! Another good shortcut is the local search facility on Yahoo! – go to the homepage and click on 'local' or go directly to **uk.local.yahoo.com/** and type 'primary schools' in the 'search for' box, and the area you wish to have a look around in the 'location' box. You can also try **www.schoolportal.co.uk** – not all primary schools are listed here, but it's still worth a browse – and you can get some good ideas for your school website too.

Languages of the World

Language	Number of speakers	Source
1 French		
2 Spanish		
3 Japanese		
4 Urdu		
5 English		
6 Italian		
7 Arabic		
8 Punjabi		
9 German		
10 Mandarin Chinese		
11 Portuguese		
12 Russian		
13 Welsh		
14 Turkish		
15 Polish		
16 Tagalog		
17 Dutch		
18 Bengali		
19 Greek		
20 Swedish		

What other languages can you think of that we can add to this list? Write them down in the box below:

Worksheet 10

French for Every Day – le français pour tous les jours

The primary school day offers limitless opportunities for practising French, and you can introduce it very easily into the everyday life of the classroom, and the school. Even if your French is rusty, there are still lots of things you can do to create a French ambiance!

Using French as a means of communication in the classroom and the school

On parle français ici . . .

You can embed as much or as little target language as you like into the life and look of your classroom. Pupils will follow your lead in this, and if you encourage its use from the start, blending French and English in display, and encourage pupils to 'stick with it', it will soon become normal practice for them. At the beginning, you might decide to repeat in English everything you say in French – I think this is a good idea, and ensures that all pupils will know what you mean – but don't be tempted to keep on doing that – then the pupils might get lazy, and if they know the English is on its way, will try to avoid processing the French you are using! Make your room as 'French' as possible, starting with the door – put a welcome sign on it – 'salut et bienvenue à la classe 4B'. You can add anything you like, such as 'visitez un petit coin de la France avec nous' or 'ici on parle français', ' ici on parle le français, l'arabique et l'anglais' – include all the languages spoken by pupils in the class. Put up a welcome sign in reception, listing all the languages that are spoken in your school.

Create a 'French corner' in your classroom, perhaps in a carpeted area if you have one – *notre coin français* – and involve the pupils in decorating it. Ask them what kinds of things they'd like to see in their *coin français*, and remind them that only French may be spoken when they are in there. Display books about France and the French language there. Don't limit the *coin français* to your classroom – have a small section of the school library devoted to books and resources about France and French – or extend it to a languages section, and include a number of different languages. Go to **www.google.fr/** or **fr.yahoo.com/** – print out the home page (page d'accueil – *accueil* literally means welcome or reception) and display. If the content doesn't look suitable, choose a French children's website.

To decorate your corner with a literacy angle, go to **www.amazon.fr** and type in 'livres pour enfants' or 'poésie pour enfants' (try Jacques Prévert, Pierre Probst, or Jacques Charpentreau if time is limited) – scroll down and choose a book with a relevant title and a visually attractive cover – print the cover out ('aggrandissez cette image', right click, print) and laminate it for a poster. Choose an English author, Eric Carle (*La Chenille qui fait des trous*), Michael Rosen and Helen Oxenbury (*La Chasse à l'ours*), J. K. Rowling (*Harry Potter et le prisonnier d'Azkaban*, *Harry Potter et la chambre des secrets* etc.!), or try any authors or titles that are on your Year Group's reading list – they may well be translated into French – then display the cover of the book in French – pupils enjoy seeing books they know in other languages.

To explore French children's writers, have a browse through **www.evene.fr/celebre/ categorie/litterature-jeunesse.php** or take some time to conduct a general search on **books.google.fr/** (the Google 'recherche de livres' search engine) or **books.google. co.uk**.

There are a number of excellent books on France written for children – try the Destination Detectives series (**www.raintreepublishers.co.uk**), the Travel Through series (**www.qed-publishing.co.uk**) or the Living in . . . series (Franklin Watts, **www. wattspub.co.uk/fwidx.htm**). These work equally well as information sources for children and for busy teachers! Put them on display in the school library or in your classroom.

Using French to communicate: where do we start?

You don't have to think in terms of 'what can I say in French?' or 'what do I want the pupils to say in French? – it's better to think in terms of 'how can we communicate effectively in French?' First and foremost, the pupils have to understand you – when they don't, both behaviour and motivation can slide. Secondly, you have to encourage them to use the language too – if you use it as often as you can, you will be setting pupils a good example!

Bear these points in mind:

- Speaking French in the classroom is easier than you might think!
- Keep things simple – if you are not yet wholly confident about your command of French, don't try to use complex sentences when a single word will do – if you struggle, so will the pupils. Remember that, in many circumstances, single words can convey a message more effectively than a long drawn-out sentence – a short sharp 'silence, s'il vous plaît!' works wonders.
- Use display as a real learning tool – think about what you might display over the year, and what purpose the display(s) will serve – remind pupils the displays are there to keep things fresh in their memory (and to help win games!).
- Be consistent with your use of French – when you know the pupils understand you, try not to slip back into English!
- Be equally consistent with what you expect from the pupils – don't let them use English, when they know the French.
- French can and does become an appropriate and accepted part of classroom routine.
- Using French as much as possible:
  - helps pupils to perceive the language as a real means of communication and maximizes opportunities for hearing and practising the language – outside the classroom they will have relatively little, if any, opportunity.
  - reinforces basic language skills.
  - builds confidence in both teacher and pupils.

Promoting teacher and pupil use of the target language

Pupils will need to practise the range of language you expect them to use – generally they will pick it up very quickly, particularly if you insist on it! You can structure parts of lessons around 'classroom language', using various games and activities to embed it. Visual displays are very useful as prompts, and don't be tempted to write all these yourself – you can devise a series of four-skill activities with visual displays – either mono or bilingual – as the goal.

Encourage your pupils to speak to each other in the target language as well, but make sure you provide them with opportunity to practise doing so – particularly practise in asking questions. I've found a good way of starting this is to get the pupils thinking about the kind of language they use a lot in the classroom – either with the teacher, or with each other, then work together on the French – in essence, building a whole lesson around target language use in the classroom. Get them used to calling you *vous* but each other *tu*, unless they're talking to more than one person at a time!

Encourage the pupils to use phrases such as:

- puis-je aller aux toilettes? (may I go to the toilet?)
- puis-je avoir un crayon? (may I have a pencil?)
- comment dit-on . . . en français? (how do you say . . . in French?)
- j'ai fait mes devoirs. (I've done my homework)
- j'ai gagné! (I've won!)

Try the following list of 'classroom questions and answers' – remember at the beginning to model the kind of response you would like the pupils to use – these and more examples of classroom language are available in the pronunciation guide (download from **www.continuumbooks.com/resources/97808264988960**).

Classroom questions and answers

- avez-vous fini? oui/non/presque (have you finished? (plural) yes, no, nearly)
- as-tu fini? (have you finished?) (singular)
- qui a fini? moi madame/monsieur/pas encore (who's finished? me Miss/Sir, not yet)
- quelle est la date aujourd'hui? lundi 17 septembre (the date in French just has the number, not a 'th'!)
- vous comprenez? tu comprends? (do you understand?)
- oui je comprends, non, je ne comprends pas (yes I understand, no I don't understand)
- êtes-vous prêts? es-tu prêt(e)? (are you ready?)
- qui peut expliquer . . . ? (who can explain . . . ?) moi Madame/Monsieur (I can Miss/Sir)
- qui peut expliquer les règles du jeu? (who can explain the rules of the game?)
- avez-vous un crayon/un stylo/des ciseaux Madame/Monsieur? (do you have a pencil/a pen/some scissors Miss/Sir?)
- as-tu . . . (when a pupil is asking another pupil) (do you have . . . ?)

Grammar point

Puis-je comes from *pouvoir*, 'to be able to'. The normal *je* form is *peux*, but when you ask a question, and invert the verb, it becomes *puis-je*, not *peux-je*.

Telling the time – l'heure

It's a good idea to teach pupils how to tell the time in French – for younger pupils, it offers opportunity to reinforce telling the time in English as well as a great way of practising numbers, and for all pupils there are many ways you can meaningfully embed telling the time into teaching and learning activities in French.

Teaching tip

Make sure pupils have grasped the 12-hour clock before you move onto the 24-hour clock. Don't be tempted to introduce o'clock, half past, quarter to and past, and all the other permutations at once – even with older children. Don't bombard pupils with 'telling the time' – stick to o'clocks, then gradually over a period of time introduce half pasts, practise those together with o'clocks, take a break from telling the time, then come back to it, recapping o'clocks and half pasts, then moving on to quarter to and past, and so on.

To keep pupils engaged, make sure you give them something to do with the time. I like to link it to the school day in the first instance, adding the time next to the day's agenda on the board. Talk about what you're all going to be doing today in French: à dix heures nous allons faire du sport; à midi et demi nous allons manger le déjeuner, and so on. Link the time to daily routine (Je me réveille à 7h 30, je me lève à 7h 45 and so on). If pupils are working on planning a trip to France, encourage them to include times of buses, trains, planes, boats and so on.

Always greet each other in French in and outside the classroom . . . When you're doing the register, after calling each name, and getting a response (oui Madame/Monsieur), ask the pupil how he/she is – you don't have to do this every day, as pupils may soon get bored with it, and it's also quite time-consuming – vary this by encouraging pupils to ask each other how they are. You can also introduce new 'feeling' words this way – for example a big yawn to denote *je suis fatigué(e)*. Ask the pupils: qui est absent aujourd'hui? every now and then, as they're generally very keen to tell you who is – and what might be wrong with them!

Instead of writing the day and date in English on the board, write it in French: lundi dix janvier 2008.

Other ideas

- Ask whose birthday it is today (qui a l'anniversaire aujourd'hui?) and sing 'Happy Birthday' to them (see the section on songs for 'Happy Birthday' in French).

- Add the day's timetable, with the times you'll be doing each activity/subject.
- Describe the weather first thing in the morning, and note that on the board (e.g. il pleut ce matin) then after lunch, if the weather's changed, make a note of that too (il fait beau cet après-midi) – pupils taking it in turns to do the writing.

Managing classroom behaviour in French

Reinforcing your classroom code of conduct, and issuing everyday classroom instructions can be done quite easily in French. You may sometimes feel that you lack sufficient language to do this, but by keeping things simple most situations can be handled in French. A stern look, coupled with a forceful 'non!', and you'll get the message across.

Classroom instructions

This could be an endless list! Here are some suggestions – don't forget to ask your pupils what they consider to be the most frequently used classroom instructions – that can be very illuminating! There is a more detailed list in the 'In the Classroom' vocabulary bank.

- ne criez pas/ne crie pas (don't shout out)
- levez la main/lève la main (put your hand(s) up)
- rangez-vous (en silence)! (line up (in silence))
- rangez vos affaires (tidy up)
- ramassez vos choses maintenant s'il vous plait (gather your things together now please)
- mettez les chaises sur les tables (put the chairs on the tables)
- fermez/ouvrez vos livres (close/open your books)

Le règlement (intérieur) de la classe or le code be bonne conduite or conseil de classe

You can use either term for 'code of conduct' – I prefer *le code de bonne conduite* as it's easily recognizable from the English, and has a nicer 'ring' to it!

Try some of these ideas for a code of conduct in French – you could write some of them on a banner, and hang up at the front of the class, or on the classroom door. I've used the pronoun *on* – although the exact translation is 'one' in English – something we don't use often in everyday speech, it's very common in French to use *on* instead of *nous* to denote 'we'. You might prefer to use *nous*, in which case the verb will be conjugated slightly differently.

- soyez toujours polis et respectueux, sois toujours poli/e et respectueux/se (be polite and respectful at all times)
- on est toujours conscient des sensibilités des autres (we are always aware of other people's feelings)
- l'intimidation n'est pas tolérée ici (we don't tolerate bullying)
- on ne permet pas l'intimidation ici (we don't allow bullying here)
- on ne triche jamais ici (we never cheat)
- on dit toujours la verité (we always tell the truth)
- on dit toujours s'il vous plaît/s'il te plaît et merci (we always say please and thank you)
- on est toujours prêt à aider les autres (we are always ready to help others)
- on ne se moque jamais des autres (we never make fun of others)
- on travaille ensemble pour réussir (we work together to succeed)
- chacun a son talent (everyone has his/her own talent)
- chacun a quelque chose à offrir (everyone has something to offer)
- notre salle de classe est un endroit sûr et heureux pour tout le monde (our classroom is a safe and happy place for everyone)
- ici on est toujours sain et sauf (we're always safe and sound here)
- il faut partager! (share and share alike!)

Activity

If you are going to be working with your class on issues surrounding racism and racial or religious intolerance, you could design some very simple, but effective posters, using headings such as *vive la différence!* or *on fête la différence!*. Some teachers prefer to avoid the use of the word *différence*, so you could try something very simple like: on est tous des êtres humains (we are all human beings). Asking pupils what they think about intolerance can give you good ideas for posters on the topic. Plan a series of art lessons around the topic and get the pupils to design posters themselves, labelling them in French themselves. These posters would look good across the school, in the corridors, or the assembly hall or reception area . . . Work with other members of staff and classes to write a school code of conduct in French and display around the school – code de bonne conduite à notre école.

Teaching tip

If your French is fairly advanced, involve the older pupils in writing their own classroom code of conduct in English, then work with them translating it into French, using bilingual dictionaries if you have them, or an online bilingual dictionary.

Everyday and seasonal greetings! – Les salutations!

This is a simple but effective way of using French as an everyday means of communication – don't forget to use these outside the classroom too.

- salut! (slightly less formal, which I tend to use outside the classroom) (hi!)
- bonjour! (hello!)
- I always add: comment ça va?
- au revoir!
- à bientôt! à tout à l'heure! (see you soon!)
- à demain (see you tomorrow)
- à la semaine prochaine (see you next week)

Expressions of praise – expressions de louange

Praising pupils' efforts is one of the easiest ways of using the target language in the classroom:

- merveilleux! (marvellous!)
- effort magnifique! (magnificent effort!)
- bon travail! (good work!)

Do the 'thumbs up' gesture too, for some added emphasis. Don't forget: you can use these for their written work too.

Journal de classe

Activity

Pupils can create their own class 'diary' which can include the weekly/daily timetable, homework timetable, dates for special events/trips and other useful information. A small A5 exercise book works well, or pupils can design a journal in Word or Publisher. The front cover can include their name, their class name, and the words 'Journal de classe'. The first page might follow a template, such as:

- prénom (first name)
- nom (family name)
- nom de l'école
- adresse de l'école
- téléphone de l'école
- classe
- professeur
- année scolaire (school year)

Another useful page is the contents page – 'sommaire'. Pupils can complete their timetable in French – horaire/emploi du temps. Think about developing a homework timetable – horaire de devoirs – this also works well on a weekly basis as a way of keeping track of homework – provide pupils with a sheet every Monday morning, with a box for each day, specifying the homework, and a small line where parents can sign to say the homework is done.

For example: semaine débutant le 26 septembre (week commencing . . .):

lundi:	maths _____ signature des parents
mardi:	anglais _____ signature des parents
mercredi:	orthographie _____ signature des parents
jeudi:	histoire _____ signature des parents
vendredi:	lecture anglais _____ signature des parents

Include a box for comments or questions by parents: commentaires/questions.

Have a short discussion about the primary curriculum, and what subjects are covered in school – asking pupils for their opinions on why they think particular subjects are included in the curriculum brings forth some rather interesting comments! Introduce the words for school subjects, and ask pupils what they like or dislike – tu aimes les maths? Oui, j'aime les maths . . . Non, je n'aime pas les maths – this is also a good opportunity to introduce some adjectives – interesting, fun and boring (intéressant, amusant et ennuyeux, with correct adjectival agreement) never go amiss as a start! Look at the class timetable in English, and as a whole group, rewrite it in French – display the French timetable (emploi/horaire du temps) prominently.

Certificates of achievement – certificats d'excellence

These always go down well with pupils, and you can create really attractive ones in Publisher – if you're not too confident with Publisher, then Word will do! For doing really well in French, use the sentence: Certificat d'excellence dans l'apprentissage de la langue française. For doing well in football, use a simple sentence like: pour un effort incroyable/merveilleux au foot. For particularly good homework, devoirs première classe. It's worth playing around with Publisher, as creating *certificats d'excellence* makes for an engaging pupil activity. Download **Worksheet 11: Certificat d'excellence dans l'apprentissage de la langue française** as an example.

Activity

Design a report template in French to send to parents and stick into pupils' workbooks towards the end of the school year – one side of A4, with the school's name and the heading 'Bulletin annuel'. Include sections for *nom d'élève, l'année scolaire, classe*. In a table, include a comment for every subject – for example a column for *discplines* (subject), a column for *appréciations et recommandations des profs* (teachers' comments, but in more poetic language!) You might write something like: sciences – bon effort, mais un peu bavard! (good effort, but a little chatty!); dessin – un véritable Monet!; français – toujours travailleur (always hard-working). Try *résultats excellents – continue comme ça!* or *attention à l'orthographe* ('a little more attention to spelling' or *à la lecture* – 'to reading'). 'Bonne participation!' Give pupils a copy of their report and encourage them to read it, and work out the comments. This can lead to some nice discussions about whether the comments are fair – something you might not be able to do with 'real' reports! Adding a column for 'effort – notes sur 10' (marks out of 10 for effort) also works well. Get parents or carers, and pupils to add their comments – English allowed! Have a look at **Worksheet 12: Bulletin Annuel** to give you some ideas, or use as a template – if you do any other subjects or activities not specifically included on the bulletin, add them in the box 'autres disciplines'.

For French, design a 'fiche d'évaluation trimestrielle' – a termly evaluation report – similar to an achievement certificate, but with a slightly more 'academic' edge! Include headings such as *évaluation d'effort (notes sur 10)*, *évaluation de prononciation*, *évaluation de lire en français* and so on.

Display a termly objectives sheet prominently. Use **Worksheet 13: Nos objectifs trimestriels pour le cours de français**, which is given in both English and French, to get you started. Which objectives would be appropriate for your developing programme of French language learning? Involve pupils in determining reasonable objectives – asking them what they'd like to be able to do in French can be very illuminating!

Wet playtime! – La recrée mouillée!

Activity

Keep children occupied with French-themed artwork, making domino cards with questions/answers/words/phrases etc. they know. In **Worksheet 14: Dominoes Template**, pupils simply fill in the various boxes with the words from the particular topic you want to work on. Remember, they'll probably need a word reference bank to help them, and some idea of how to play dominoes!

Play French music during wet playtime – pupils can hum along and join in!

Building vocabulary

It's important to avoid a purely vocabulary-driven approach to language teaching – without a context to use the vocabulary in, or the necessary structures to bind the words together into meaning, they will simply not embed new words, nor make any real progress as a language learner. Equally though, in order to engage in conversation, and make language rich and varied, pupils do need to build a certain baseline vocabulary, and be encouraged to keep adding to it. Map out a 'conversation route' first (see 'Building conversation') and decide which units of vocabulary will be core to that topic, which will be additionally offered to more able pupils, and the types of conversation you can use to practise the vocabulary. Make things as relevant to pupils' worlds as possible – if you're going to be talking sports for example, find out what sports they like, and know something about, and make that your starting point.

Teaching tip

Little and often works best – encourage pupils to work on a small number of words regularly, rather than a huge list once a month!

Vocabulary book – mon carnet de vocabulaire

Activity

Children will benefit from having their own reference bank of words, and from the opportunity to both write and read words. It's also a simple, but effective, introduction to using a bilingual dictionary. From Year 3, give each pupil a suitable exercise book, and for homework, ask them to decorate it . . . Give younger pupils some ideas of the kinds of ways they could decorate their *carnet*, such as finding ClipArt pictures or copyright-free images on the Web that they can download, cut out carefully, and glue onto the front cover:

- French or EU flags
- famous French landmarks
- French foods such as croissants or baguettes
- euro notes and coins

Encourage them to find pictures of France, and cut those out too – perhaps go to the local travel agents and ask for some brochures on France. Choose a book from the library, and carefully trace a picture from there, then colour it in. Spend some time in art and design lessons working together on ideas. Give some sample phrases they can use, and either write them carefully by hand, or experiment with 'fancy fonts' on a computer:

- J'adore le français!
- le français – c'est super!
- mon premier dictionnaire anglais-français

Work out how you'd like the *carnet* to work and give the pupils explicit instructions on how to set it up. For example, will the lead word be in English or in French? Will each page be for a single letter of the alphabet, or will you combine certain letters on individual pages, such as x,y,z? How many pages per letter? Will pupils have to draw a line with a ruler down the middle of the page, or just fold the page in half?

You may like to create your own *carnet de vocabulaire* first to show pupils as an example. Plan ahead for how you'd like the pupils to use their carnet – do you want them to write every single word they learn in it, or will you select certain ones? Remember you'll probably need at least five minutes for pupils to add a couple of words to their *carnet* – when you know you are going to be working on the *carnet*, get a pupil to hand them out at the beginning of the lesson.

Pupils can decorate the cover – encourage them to think of French ideas for decoration – from words such as 'le français – c'est super!' and 'La belle France' to images such as *Mariane* and *le Tricolore*.

 Teaching tip

Introduce 'our word of the day' – notre mot du jour – choosing a series of individual words to learn over a period of time. You can keep this on the board all day, and at various times prompt the pupils to repeat it, and say what it means in English. On Friday afternoons, have a *petit quiz* (oral or written), with a *bonbon* or a sticker for those who remember all five. At the end of each month, see who can remember them all! If there's time, get the pupils to write each *mot du jour* in their *carnet de vocabulaire*.

For example:

Qu-est-ce que c'est, notre mot du jour aujourd'hui?

Et ça veut dire quoi en anglais?

Croque mots – a croque monsieur with a difference!

Activity

Fold a piece of A4 in half lengthways. Draw a baguette on one side of the paper, making sure there's enough room for 5–10 words on it. Depending on the number of words you'd like your pupils to focus on, write them out with the English equivalent – if it's a noun, include the gender; if it's a verb, include the infinitive and the *je/tu* form; if it's an adjective include the masculine and feminine form. You've now got a *croque mots*. Photocopy the required number of baguettes, and give each pupil a *croque* at the beginning of the week, asking them to make sure they learn them for Friday afternoon (vendredi après-midi) ready for the *quiz de croque*. Display a *Galerie de croques* around the room, or in the corridors – after a term, you'll have an impressive *croque* collection, and an even more impressive one at the end of the school year, which also serves as a constant reminder to pupils, and as an evolving vocabulary bank. **Worksheet 15: Croque mots** is provided to give you an idea of how this works, and there's a blank template too (**Worksheet 16**)

Mon profil

Activity

As pupils begin to build a baseline vocabulary, they can design profiles of themselves for display either in the classroom or across the school – these are also useful for info swap with partner schools overseas. Even with very limited vocabulary, these make for a fantastic display, and certainly catch the attention of all pupils, staff and visitors if displayed prominently near the reception area – particularly if there are pupil photos attached . . .

As a title, I like to use 'Mon profil', though you can also use *me voilà* or *me voici* – even just *moi* is OK!

Younger pupils may benefit from a profile template that you design, with specified areas of information. Older children can brainstorm ideas of what to include to encourage them to reflect on what they have learnt. **Worksheet 17: Moi!** and **Worksheet 18: All about me!** give a basic template you can photocopy, both in French and in English.

The profile displays work especially well if there is a photograph attached – pupils can either bring one in, or you can link some ICT work into the profile if you have access to a school digital camera. After securing the necessary permissions, pupils can take headshots of each other, download as a JPEG or GIF file, and insert into their profile. Alternatively, they can scan their photograph, save the scanned file appropriately, and insert that into the profile. This is an option even if you don't have a digital camera. Include a box with the instruction 'colle ici ta photo' if you prefer to glue photographs in, or 'insère ici ta photo' for 'insert your photo here'. Use 'Mon profil' as a way of introducing adjectives – brainstorm adjectives that describe personalities in English first, as this encourages pupils to think about the qualities they like in their friends, and the kind of things they don't like. It also encourages them to think about their own strengths, and any weaknesses they may have! Try some of the following:

- cool, sportif/sportive (sporty)
- paresseux/paresseuse (lazy)
- égoïste (selfish)
- généreux/généreuse
- fort/forte en foot (good at football)
- charmant/charmante
- intelligent/intelligente
- sympa (generally nice!)
- conformiste
- assuré/assurée (confident)
- timide (shy)
- individualiste
- riche
- assez sûr(e) de soi
- parfait, etc.

Pupils can be encouraged to design their own profile design in English first – this gets them thinking about the kinds of things that they'd like to be able to say in French – if it's important in English, it's important in French too, and gives a sense of relevance to the language they are learning.

Building conversation

It's always good practice to work on building conversation in the target language regularly and consistently. The age group of the pupils will dictate the speed at which you can introduce and embed new language, as well as the range and extent of language you can use, and more importantly, be confident that the pupils will also be able to assimilate and produce for themselves. Providing pupils with authentic conversational scenarios is crucial – if they don't see the relevance in what they're saying or asking about, you may find that motivation drops alarmingly!

You may decide to follow a prescribed course with your pupils (remember to browse the NACELL website for recommended resources), but if you are starting French without a course (don't forget to look at the QCA SoW for ideas!), think about topics you can cover that your pupils will realistically be able to engage in a conversation about, with you, with each other, and hopefully with their new French pals! Try the following:

- Greetings – salut, bonjour, etc.
- Comment ça va? Très bien merci (or not so well!) – you can ask pupils how they are simply by using the phrase Ça va? but I prefer to use Comment ça va? at first so that we can start to build up a bank of 'question words' (interrogative pronouns) in French. Give pupils an initial choice of about three or four different responses – they can add to these gradually as their vocabulary builds up.
- Name – Comment t'appelles-tu? Je m'appelle . . .
- Où habites-tu? J'habite à . . . en . . . (towns, countries, flags, colours, etc.).
- Quel âge as-tu? J'ai . . . ans/Quelle est la date aujourd'hui? Lundi, 18 janvier (numbers, days, months, birthdays).
- Quel est ton numéro de téléphone? (new identity, with French phone number, e.g. 22-34-58-91).
- Quelles langues parles-tu? Anglais, français, farsi (languages, countries, nationalities, adjectives).
- Quel temps fait-il? Il fait . . . (weather, adjectives, etc.).
- Quelles sont tes matières préférées? (school subjects, timetable, j'adore, j'aime, je n'aime pas, je détèste).
- My healthy-eating diary (food and drink, shopping, debate on what 'healthy eating' is, role-play café, etc.).
- Sports and other hobbies (likes, dislikes, free time, healthy living, etc.).
- Musical instruments (music, musicians, orchestras, musical composition, etc.).
- Family (names, family tree, animals).

- Notre salle de classe (classroom) and school environment – classroom objects, what we use them for, what makes a nice environment to work in. Don't forget, good debate or discussion in English is also sound learning, and part of the Primary National Strategy – so don't avoid topics that you think pupils can't engage with in French – they can debate or discuss in English, and choose key words in French to create simple sentences on the topic: Je pense que/Je trouve que (I think that); A mon avis (in my opinion); parce que (because); and link with a bilingual dictionary speed quiz to build vocabulary.

Role Play

Activity

Use role-play as a means of getting pupils to engage in longer exchanges, and to hone their writing and drama skills. You can start off really simply, and pupils can themselves put together short plays with even very limited baseline language. Set some scenarios such as 'Meeting someone new' or 'In the café' – show an example, and make it slightly more complex than they'd be able to produce on their own, and then encourage pupils to think of what they do know, and how to get the message across. In pairs or small groups, pupils come up with characters and names, and create short, easily memorable dialogues – try not to let them use their written script – this then becomes reading, rather than acting and speaking!

Example: faire la connaissance de quelqu'un

Peter: Salut! Enchanté!

Amélie: Salut! Comment ça va?

Peter: Très bien merci! Et toi?

Amélie: Très bien!

Peter: Je m'appelle Alphonse. Comment t'appelles-tu?

Amélie: Je m'appelle Amélie, et j'habite à Limoges.

Peter: Limoges! C'est une ville magnifique!

Amélie: Où habites-tu?

Peter: J'habite à Manchester, dans le nord-ouest de l'Angleterre.

Amélie: J'adore Manchester! A bientôt!

Peter: A bientôt!

Example: au café Descartes

Serveur: Bonjour Madame!

Madame: Bonjour! Je voudrais la carte, s'il vous plaît.

Serveur: Bien sûr Madame! Voilà!

(*2 minutes plus tard*)

Serveur: Vous avez fait votre choix Madame? Que désirez-vous?

Madame: Je voudrais une grande crêpe au citron, s'il vous plaît.

Serveur: Oui Madame! Vous désirez quelque chose à boire?

Madame: Oui, une tasse de chocolat chaud, s'il vous plaît

(*10 minutes plus tard*)

Madame: L'addition s'il vous plaît.

Serveur: Bien sûr Madame, ça fait onze euros.

Madame: Voilà, et au revoir!

Serveur: Merci Madame et bonne journée!

Other scenarios might include: chez le docteur (great for miming illnesses); faire des courses; en vacances; à la recherche de l'Europe – ask pupils for their suggestions too.

Create a set, and use props and costumes wherever possible – pupils really do get into the 'act'! Save all the scripts they make, revisiting them as the year progresses, encouraging pupils to add to the dialogue. Compile a *dossier de théâtre* and use these for performances at French Day, or at any other occasion where you have parents and visitors at school. Remember to take photos, and display these too. Include lots of pair work 'chatting' – asking and answering questions.

Je fais une promenade en ville – get the pupils up and about – they're walking around town on a Saturday morning, bumping into friends and chatting to them – specify the minimum number of questions they have to ask each other.

Building a repertoire of songs

Activity

This activity can be worked on across the whole of KS2, finishing with a flourish as the outgoing Year 6 put on a special performance for pupils and parents, for guests on the French Day (or Week), or even pupils and teachers at a selection of secondary schools. The performances can be filmed, or audio recorded. Encourage pupils to create a song book – *notre livre de chansons, notre collection de chansons* or *nos plus belles chansons d'enfants*, putting the date on each song sheet they design so that they can look back from the lofty heights of Year 6 to their work in Year 3 – but be careful that the lyrics they are reproducing are not still under copyright. Start by brainstorming favourite children's songs, rhymes and poems in English, and repeat this as the children progress through KS2, so that you have a parallel bank of English works. Ask pupils if they know any French pieces, or set a small fact-finding homework for them – most parents and guardians will know 'Frère Jacques' and 'Sur le pont d'Avignon' to get the ball rolling. It's quite nice to start with 'Frère Jacques', as this can be worked on in music lessons too, encouraging pupils to sing in the round. Singing in the round works wonders for concentration and listening skills, and sounds absolutely lovely as well.

Frère Jacques, Frère Jacques

Dormez-vous? Dormez-vous?
Sonnez les matines! Sonnez les matines!
Din, dan, don! Din, dan, don!

Have a look at the 'Frère Jacques' entry on Wikipedia – there is a small image of the musical notes matched to the words, which can be used in display or in music lessons).

Songs are musical stories, so I always discuss the story of songs with pupils – this one tells the story of the young monk Brother Jacques whose job is to ring the bells for morning prayers (les matines), but who oversleeps, and gets into trouble! Children pick up the French words very quickly, so play the song if you have a CD or access to it via the Web, or sing it, and they'll soon join in, particularly if you do a quick 'spoken' run-through first, with lots of miming of being asleep, and ringing bells. Explain what singing in the round is, then divide the class into three groups, and launch in – you'll probably have to be quite a strict conductor at first! As the class gets more used to singing in this way, make the groups smaller. Don't forget to use mime and gesture as you introduce songs – knock on Jacques's bedroom door, put your head on your arms as though you're sleeping, wag your finger, then chime bells with expansive arm movements – many children pick up and retain the words far quicker when they can associate gesture with language.

'Frère Jacques' is a very useful tune, and works well with any number of topics. Use it to practise days and numbers in the first instance and, as pupils begin to extend their vocabulary, have little small-group competitions to see who can come up with the best new lyrics – individual words will do, according to the topic you're working on. Try greetings (bonjour, salut; bonjour, salut; au revoir, au revoir; bonne nuit, bonne nuit; bonsoir, bonsoir) to start them off.

Some classic French children's songs include:

- 'Sur le pont d'Avignon'
- 'Alouette, gentille alouette'
- 'Il était un petit navire'
- 'Meunier, tu dors'
- 'Savez-vous planter les choux?'
- 'Au clair de la lune'
- 'En passant par la Lorraine'

Browse through the alphabetical list on **www.momes.net/comptines/comptines-chansons.html** and choose a song or rhyme according to what you're working on; there are a lot of categories, including animals, colours, people, and number and spelling songs, many with both the lyrics and music. Don't worry if only the lyrics are available, either do a further search (for example: **www.fr.yahoo.com**, search term 'musique Frère Jacques') or use the lyrics as a rhyme or poem, rather than a song. Most of the pages have a printable version, 'version imprimable', so they're easy to print out for display, as part of a musical collage, or as a song sheet – though you may have to make the font size bigger.

Browse these sites for ideas – many also have audio files:
www.momes.net
comptine.free.fr/
www.uptoten.com/enfants/boowakwala-navigation-gamesindex.html
www.comptine-enfants.com/

For a more global perspective, try **www.mamalisa.com/world/** – you can view the site in English, French or Spanish, and there are songs from around the world in either sheet music form and/or MP3 format. Other songs you might like to investigate to start you off are: 'Joli tambour'; 'Ah les crocodiles'; 'Ainsi font, font, font'; 'Le Mois de mai'; 'Nous n'irons plus au bois'; 'Lundi matin'; 'C'est la mère Michel'; 'Maan les p'tits bateaux'; 'J'ai perdu le do de ma clarinette'; 'Le Bon Roi Dagobert'; 'Un, deux, trois, allons dans le bois'; 'A la claire fontaine'; 'Roule galette'; 'Il était un petit navire'; 'Colchiques dans les prés'; 'Dodo l'enfant do'; 'Il était une bergère'; 'Pomme de reinette'; 'Une souris verte'; 'Il court, il court le furet'; 'Auprès de ma blonde'; 'Tape, tape, petite main'.

Activity

In your PE lessons, combine singing with dancing! These are some popular 'rondes': 'Mademoiselle voulez-vous'; 'Il était un fermier'; 'Ron, ron macaron'; 'J'aime la galette'; 'Bonjour ma cousine' – for a comprehensive list, browse through **www.momes.net/comptines/comptines-danses.html** – I've used several (for example 'Dansons la capucine'; 'P'tite mademoiselle'; 'Il tourne en rond notre beau bateau') and searched for clips on YouTube France for choreography ideas!

It's always interesting to compare songs and rhymes in English and French – try 'Le Fermier dans son pré' or 'Les Roues du bus' – I play about with translations to practise whatever particular words we're working on, though there are sure to be other versions! Again, encourage pupils to come up with their own versions:

Le fermier dans son pré

Le fermier dans son pré
Un, deux, trois
Le fermier dans son pré
Le fermier a un chien
Le fermier a un chien
Quatre, cinq, six
Le fermier a un chien
Le fermier a des canards
Le fermier a des canards
Sept, huit, neuf
Le fermier a des canards

Les roues du bus tournent en rond

Tournent en rond
Tournent en rond
Les roues du bus tournent en rond
Toute la journée

Le chauffeur du bus crie

Calmez-vous !
Calmez-vous !
Calmez-vous !
Le chauffeur du bus crie
Calmez-vous !
Toute la journée

Les bébés dans le bus font

Wah-wah-wah (children pinch noses to get a really nasal sound to this)
Wah-wah-wah
Wah-wah-wah
Les bébés dans le bus font
Wah-wah-wah
Toute la journée

Activity

'Head and shoulders' lends itself very well to whole-group translation, as well as for designing a bilingual song sheet – see **Worksheet 19: Tête et épaules** as an example. Pupils create a two-column table, writing the lyrics in English in one column, and in French in the other column. Raise the level of challenge, and encourage them to 'hide' the table when they have finished designing the song sheet, preferably with an appropriate image (ClipArt has a wonderful selection of dancing skeletons!) so that it doesn't appear on the finished product (left-click on the table, format, borders and shading, select 'none', apply to table).

The French lyrics are:

Tête, épaules, genoux, et pieds

Tête, épaules, genoux, et pieds
Yeux, oreilles, bouche et nez
Tête, épaules, genoux, et pieds

If you've worked on musical notes, in your music lesson, put the pupils into small groups, and get them to work out possible notes for the tune. Piano (with the notes stuck onto keys as an aide-memoire if necessary), xylophone and glockenspiel (some have the notes engraved or marked on the bars) are great instruments for this activity.

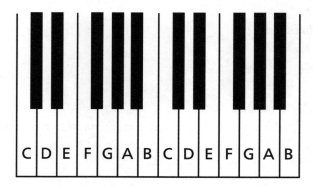

Younger children enjoy 'Two little dicky birds', which also works well as a bilingual reading text, comparing similarities and differences in the English and French versions, and how rhyme and rhythm work – for example notice how in the English version, Peter and Paul are told to fly away first, then come back, yet in the French version, it's the other way round – the rhythm simply works better in each language that way round!

Two little dicky birds	*Deux petits oiseaux*
Sitting on a wall	*Assis sur une branche*
One named Peter	*L'un s'appelle Pierre*
One named Paul	*L'autre s'appelle Paul*
Fly away Peter	*Viens-t'en Pierre!*
Fly away Paul	*Viens-t'en Paul!*
Come back Peter	*Va-t-en Pierre!*
Come back Paul	*Va-t-en Paul!*

See if there are any more songs you can reasonably expect your pupils to translate. Remind them that translations do not have to have exactly the same words, and that it's OK to play around with meanings when you are singing for fun. After trying 'Head and shoulders', try 'Ten green bottles' – I worked with Year 5 on the following – it's slightly different in meaning, but the rhyme is retained:

J'ai dix bouteilles vertes assises sur le mur

J'ai dix bouteilles vertes assises sur le mur
Si une bouteille verte tombe je suis sûr/e
Que j'ai neuf bouteilles vertes assises sur le mur . . .

Encourage pupils to think of tunes they know and like, and see what French they can fit to it – brainstorm favourite tunes, and the French you've already worked on together, choosing several topics, then set them to work! Greetings are always a good place to start, then moving on to other topics. One of my favourites is the days of week to the tune of *The Flintstones*!

Activity

As part of your daily routine, ask whose birthday it is, and write the names on the board. Sing 'Bon anniversaire' to the tune of 'Happy birthday', or try this traditional French birthday song:

Bon anniversaire,
Mes voeux les plus sincères
Que ces quelques fleurs
Vous apportent le bonheur
Que l'année entière
Vous soit douce et légère

Et que l'an fini
Nous soyons tous réunis
Pour chanter encore
Bon anniversaire!

In English, it reads something like this:

Happy birthday
My very best wishes to you
I hope these few flowers
Will bring you happiness and good luck
That the coming year

Will be kind to you (or bring you good things)
That when the year is over
We can all be reunited once more
To sing
Happy Birthday to you!

A simple Web search with the search term 'children's birthday song' or 'chanson pour enfants anniversaire' on either English or French language search engines will yield lots of sites where you can access various 'Happy birthday' songs. I like this one, as pupils type in their own name, and the figures on screen automatically sing the song with the pupil's name in it: **www.uptoten.com/enfants/boowakwala-birthday-birthdaysong.html**

If your school is hosting a Christmas or Nativity play, add a French flavour to the music! Try **www.momes.net/comptines/noel2/saint-nicolas2.html** for a song about St Nicholas, whose feast day is on 6 December and is a popular celebration in certain parts of France. To the tune of 'Jingle bells' try 'Vive le vent' – I learnt these lyrics, though there are probably a number of versions!

Sur le long chemin
Tout blanc de neige blanche
Un vieux monsieur s'avance
Avec sa canne dans la main
Et tout là-haut le vent
Qui siffle dans les branches
Lui souffle romance
Qu'il chantait petit enfant

Vive le vent ! Vive le vent !
Vive le vent d'hiver
Qui s'en va sifflant, soufflant
Dans les grands sapins verts
Ooooooohhhhh!
Vive le vent! Vive le vent!
Vive le temps d'hiver
Boule de neige et jour de l'an
Et bonne année grand-mère

Other popular carols are: 'Au grand Saint-Nicolas'; 'Il est né le divin enfant'; 'Mon beau sapin'; 'Douce Nuit, Sainte Nuit'; 'Petit Papa Noël'; 'Joyeux Noël'; 'le Bonhomme de Bois'; Le P'tit Renne au nez rouge'.

Encourage the pupils to design song and carol sheets, which can be displayed in the classroom or around the school.

Activity

When you're working on aspects of French culture, include an introduction to the French National Anthem (l'hymne national) – *la Marseillaise* (The Song of Marseille). Start with a general discussion on the role and function of national anthems, and a quick poll to see who actually knows ours! Many French people are terrifically proud of *la Marseillaise* – ask pupils if they think that people in this country feel the same about ours

Wikipedia has the full text in both English and French, as well as an MP3 file you can download and save, or play via the IWB. Have a look at the French President's official site on **www.elysee.fr/accueil/** – apart from having lots of video clips which are great for practising your own oral skills, if you type 'la Marseillaise' into the 'rechercher' box, you will be able to access a pdf which has the full official text, plus the sheet music.

The anthem for the EU, or European Anthem (l'hymne de l'Union Européenne) provides a nice opportunity for introducing pupils to some classical music – it's Beethoven's 'Ode to joy' ('L'Ode à la joie') – have a look at **europa.eu/abc/symbols/anthem/index_en.htm** or **www.national-anthems.net/EE** – both sites contain links to audio files of the music. Add this to your file of 'fast facts' on the EU, and include it in a general knowledge quiz at your French day – it's bound to stump most grown-ups!

There are increasingly more CD French song collections on the market, some 'traditional', and some written specifically for the primary classroom – consult **www.nacell.org.uk/resources/resources.htm** for information about these – the list isn't exhaustive, but it's a good starting place. For more ideas about songs, or rhymes and poems, have a look at 'Let's Join In!' (Cynthia Martin and Catherine Cheater) in the Young Pathfinder series on **www.cilt.org.uk/publications/ypf.htm** (this link also gives details of the entire Young Pathfinder series, which is a fantastic ideas bank for early language learning).

Songs are great motivators and learning tools – children are familiar with 'musical learning' in their first language, and are comfortable with pace, rhyme, rhythm, beat, movement and so on. Singing really does encourage active learning, and is an effective way of introducing, reinforcing and embedding new vocabulary. Songs offer an interactive and engaging way of working on pronunciation, of exploring language and rhythm, and of comparing one language to another. Exploit your songs to the full, encouraging pupils to read, write, design and create, as well as participate. Remember not to overdo the same songs – these are learning activities, and pupils will naturally tire of the same thing over and over again – it's important to keep challenging pupils, and to give them new words and music to experiment with.

Certificat d'excellence dans l'apprentissage de la langue française

_____

Élève magnifique!

French in the Primary Classroom © Angela McLachlan 2008

Bulletin Annuel

ÉTABLISSEMENT	Nom d'élève	Classe
Année scolaire	Nom de professeur	
Disciplines	*Appréciations et recommandations des professeurs*	*Évaluation d'effort (notes sur 10)*
anglais		
français		
mathématiques		
sciences		
informatique		
dessin		
histoire		
géographie		
musique		
éducation physique et sportive		
autres disciplines		
commentaires du professeur		
commentaires des parents		
commentaires d'élève		

Worksheet 12

Croque mots

janvier	January
février	February
mars	March
avril	April
mai	May
juin	June
juillet	July
le jour	day
le mois	month
je m'appelle	My name is
j'ai sept ans	I'm seven years old

French in the Primary Classroom © Angela McLachlan 2008

Moi!

mon nom: _____

mon âge: _____

colle où insère
ta photo ici!

domicile: _____

famille: _____

ma taille: _____

mon passe-temps préféré: _____

ma matière préférée: _____

ma couleur préférée: _____

mon plat préféré: _____

ma boisson préférée: _____

mon sport préféré: _____

mon film préféré: _____

mon livre préféré: _____

mon animal préféré: _____

mon joueur de foot préféré: _____

mon/ma chanteur/chanteuse préféré(e): _____

ma plus grande qualité: _____

mon pire défaut: _____

French in the Primary Classroom © Angela McLachlan 2008

Supporting Learning with French: Enhancing Literacy and ICT Skills through French

Focus on literacy

Speaking, listening, reading and writing skills can be enhanced very successfully through the medium of French, and many teachers have told me that even pupils who generally avoid either participating orally or reading and writing in English, are often keen to 'have a go' and engage in French lessons. The trick is not to overwhelm pupils with lots of language they don't understand, and to present activities as an enjoyable challenge. Try to introduce a blend of activities which include the four skills into your lessons, keeping each activity to a reasonable length. If you want to focus on enhancing literacy skills, I'd recommend you teach pupils the French alphabet very early on in their programme of learning. Not only will it help younger children remember the English alphabet, it provides opportunities for pupils of all ages to get to grips with words, phrases and sentences across all four skills.

Introducing the alphabet – l'alphabet français

Activity

You can use the much same strategies for teaching the French alphabet as you might do for teaching the English one. I generally use this sequence:
- On the board, have the letters of the alphabet ready to use as visual prompts.
- The pupils will need their mini whiteboards (or workbooks/paper) with pens ready.
- Ask the pupils to chant the English alphabet slowly and clearly.
- Now ask the children to listen very carefully (écoutez très attentivement) and recite the French alphabet to them, pointing to the letters on the board – exaggerate your mouth movements a little as this often keeps the pupils

focused on the sounds you're making (as well as the funny faces!). Ask them if they recognized any sounds, pointing to individual letters as a prompt.

- Now choose some individual letters to say in French, asking the children to listen very carefully again and guess what the letters could be in English (qui peut deviner la lettre anglaise?).
- Say several letters one after the other, picking up speed, then slowing down again, which the pupils then have to repeat in English – remember to use lots of praise for their responses (excellent, merveilleux, incroyable, que vous êtes fantastiques! etc.).
- Now repeat these steps, but instead of saying the letters, ask the children to write them down.
- Repeat the alphabet in full, again exaggerating your mouth movements a little and ask the pupils to join in when they can (you will see lots of wide open mouths, mimicking your own mouth movements).
- You start with a and go round the class, pointing to each pupil who has to say the next letter. Go out of sequence occasionally, pointing to a pupil on the other side of the room – that keeps them on their toes, and encourages them to listen carefully.
- J'écris avec mon doigt! Using a finger, spell out different words in the air, asking pupils to call out individual letters in French, then the whole word (don't forget to let them have a go as well).
- As a whole group, sing the English alphabet to the tune of 'Twinkle twinkle little star' or the army marching song if that's more their style!
- Ask the pupils if they'd like to have a go at singing the French alphabet (qui voudrait chanter l'alphabet français?). Start off, and they'll soon join in.
- Practise the French alphabet orally in short, sharp bursts over a series of lessons, rather than spending a whole lesson on it, then not revisiting it for several lessons.
- On the board, show the pupils the French alphabet, including the letters with accents, explaining that these are important in French as they tell us something about how the word should sound and look. Give some examples of words with accents: enchanté, règle, français, être, Noël.

Language point

These are the names of the accents, à, é = accent aigu; è = accent grave ;
ç = cédille ; ê, û = circonflexe, ë = tréma.

You can practise French as well as other literacy and thinking skills at the same time. Photocopy the alphabet sheet (**Worksheet 20: L'alphabet français**) and give pupils a copy each to refer to.

Try the following kinds of questions:

'Salut! Regarde l'alphabet très attentivement. Lis les questions ci-dessous et répond en français.'

('Hello! Look at the alphabet very carefully. Read the questions below and answer in French.')

'**Combien y a-t-il de consonnes en plus que de voyelles dans l'alphabet?**'
('**How many more consonants are there than vowels in the alphabet?**')

Teaching tip

Remember you don't always have to put the instructions in English as well – encourage pupils to infer meaning, and work things out for themselves too.

Example:

- Demain, c'est *mercredi*, quelle est la deuxième lettre du mot pour *today*? (Tomorrow is *mercredi*, what's the second letter of the word for *today*? (U – aujourd'hui.))
- Combien de voyelles y a-t-il? (How many vowels are there?)
- How many consonants are there? (Combien de consonnes y a-t-il?)
- Combien de voyelles y a-t-il dans le mot *maison*? (How many vowels are there in the word *maison*?)
- How many more consonants than vowels are there in the word *nourriture*?
- Quelle lettre vois-tu une fois dans le mot *chat*, deux fois dans le mot *cacher*, et pas du tout dans le mot *oiseau*? (Which letter can you see once in *chat*, twice in *cacher* and not at all in *oiseau*?)
- Aujourd'hui c'est *lundi*, quelle est la première lettre du mot pour demain?

Example: Rework simple verbal reasoning questions

Souligne le mot en paranthèses qui correspond au mot en dehors des paranthèses. Underline the word in brackets that corresponds to the word outside the brackets.

> *la chaise* (le chat, <u>le lit</u>, le livre, la voiture)

You can adapt this to suit any category of words. The above example shows 'furniture' words. You can try adjectives versus verbs for example:

> *grand* (marcher, chanter, <u>petit,</u> sourire)

or work on masculine and feminine forms of adjectives :

> grande (petit, <u>petite,</u> intéressant, vieux)

or differentiate between different verb groups, for example *-er*, *-ir* or *-re* verbs

> *regarder* (perdre, <u>oublier</u>, faire, mettre)

Je suis poète!

Activity

Encourage pupils to write a short poem about a topic you have covered. You might want to give them a title, or a series of titles they can choose from, or as a whole-group, brainstorm possible titles. Try these with the title 'Salut!'

Example: Ma chanson française!

Salut!

Salut mes copains! Ça va bien?

Moi, ça va super!

Aujourd'hui c'est lundi

Dimanche était hier!

Salut la France! Salut Paris!

Comment ça va aujourd'hui?

Quel temps fait-il maintenant chez vous?

Chez moi, j'ai froid!

Harry, Year 5

Remember it doesn't have to rhyme! Here's another offering by Harry in Year 5, under the title 'Salutations!' (Greetings)

Bonjour, bonjour!
Au revoir, au revoir!
Salut, salut
Bonsoir, bonsoir!
Bonne nuit, bonne nuit
Et bon anniversaire

You can write a poem as a whole group too, with each pupil suggesting words. Try it with favourite pastimes or school subjects, linking it to adjectives – remember to do a quick brainstorm of pastimes and adjectives first:

- j'adore jouer au foot – merveilleux!
- j'adore manger des frites – délicieux!
- je déteste ranger ma chambre – ennuyeux!

Dictation – dictée

Activity

You might remember French dictation as a rather boring way of learning French, but it can actually work very well in the primary classroom, really encouraging pupils to relate the spoken word to the written word while practising neat writing, punctuation, spelling and listening carefully all at the same time. Introduce *dictée* as a 'quiz' activity right at the beginning of your French programme, and this will also help embed the language you are teaching. Keep the *dictée* nice and short, and read slowly and clearly. You might like to do a practice run with a very short English text on the same topic first. You can differentiate *dictée* by having carousel activities – for example, see the two *dictées* below. These *dictées* are differentiated: while you are doing the less difficult *dictée* with one group (Group 1), the more able group (Group 2) can be doing the more difficult worksheet and vice versa. When the pupils are used to *dictées*, get them to prepare a short text on the particular topic you are working on – check the spelling and punctuation, and have some fun with whole-group pronunciation, then these texts can be used as *dictées* for the rest of the class. If you have access to an ICT suite, get them to record their *dictées* which other pupils can play back and complete at their leisure.

Try these to get you started – you'll find a short punctuation mark glossary in the vocabulary reference banks.

Group 1

Salut! (point d'exclamation). Je m'appelle Patric et j'ai douze ans. (point) J'habite à Paris, (virgule) la capitale de la France. (point). Mon numéro de téléphone est 22-49-56.
FIN

Group 2

Salut! (point d'exclamation). Je m'appelle Patric et j'ai douze ans. (point) J'habite à Paris, (virgule) la capitale de la France. (point). J'ai un frère, (virgule) qui s'appelle Luc, (virgule) et deux sœurs qui s'appellent Sophie et Michelle. (point) Mon numéro de téléphone est 22-49-56. Comment t'appelles-tu? (point d'interrogation)
FIN

Related activities can include reading out loud – get the pupils to read their *dictées* back to the class in their best French accent. Talk about punctuation, and where the various marks belong. Look at grammar patterns, such as the *je* form ending in *-e*. Ask Group 2 why they think there is an *-ent* on the end of *s'appellent*. Translate the texts into English, pointing out that 'word-for-word' translations often sound funny – the trick is to get the same meaning as the French words, but in English that doesn't sound a bit funny – so no 'I have 12 years' for 'I am 12 years old'!

Comprehension activities

Activity

You can give comprehension and reading activities a 'French feel'. Write or copy (where copyright allows) a text in English of appropriate length according to the year group, and ask a series of questions based on it. Download **Worksheet 21: Some Facts about France** to start you off. You could also do this as a form of shared reading, or whole-group listening, then ask the questions orally. This works well as a small-group activity too – give the pupils some time to read the text and discuss it in their groups, then have a question and answer session. Include a series of 'discussion questions' that the whole class can then talk about together.

Other related activities might include:

- Prepare a similar text about England, Scotland, Wales or Northern Ireland.
- Give pupils the text without the questions, asking them to prepare at least 10 questions based on the text.
- Give pupils the questions without the text, asking them to prepare a text based on the questions.
- Additional fact-finding – for example, what languages are spoken in Andorra, Belgium, Germany, Italy, Luxembourg, Monaco, Spain and Switzerland?

Teaching tip

Remember you can challenge more able pupils by giving the instructions, examples and questions only in French – less able pupils may feel more comfortable with the activity if you give those in English. You can always give them in both languages – but only at the beginning until pupils are more used to the language – otherwise they may simply give up reading the French, and go straight to the English. You can also let pupils respond either in English or in French – perhaps on occasion giving bonus points to those who can manage it all in French. I've found that using less 'formal' language on these kinds of worksheet activities works well in motivating pupils to engage with the activity. Give pupils a specific amount of time to complete the activity, depending on their general ability level, the level of complexity in the questions and the number of questions.

Idioms and proverbs – idiomes et proverbes

Looking at, and talking about, idioms and proverbs in French makes for a series of interesting literacy lessons. Older children, particularly Year 6, will engage with the topic with gusto. Start the lesson(s) off with input on the difference between 'idiom' and 'proverb' in English, giving a couple of examples of each.

Idiom:

An idiom is an expression or a phrase that has a different meaning from the meaning of the words in it:

- *it's a piece of cake* means 'it's really easy'
- *that rings a bell* means 'that sounds familiar'

Proverb:

A sentence that gives us advice, or tries to tell us something important; proverbs tell us things that are common sense:

- *Many hands make light work* – lots of people working together makes less work for everyone.
- *Prevention is better than cure* – it's better to avoid making a mistake in the first place if you can.

Activity

In small groups, pupils can brainstorm either proverbs or idioms, or both, then feedback to the whole group. Draw two columns on the board, noting down each one. Discuss what they actually mean – ask pupils to rewrite a series of idioms and proverbs in their own words in English – this works well as a small-group activity. Do it orally with the whole group, writing what the class considers to be the best new wording on the board.

You could also set this as a 'topic preparation' homework, asking pupils to look up both words, and find at least one example of each.

Choose examples that can fit into other things you want to talk about, such as classroom conduct: 'I'm all ears when my teacher is talking' (je suis tout oreilles quand le prof parle) or 'no sooner said than done' (aussitôt dit, aussitôt fait). Use 'practice makes perfect' (c'est en forgeant qu'on devient forgeron). Comparing English idioms and proverbs is a great way of encouraging pupils to think about how their own language works, how sometimes the 'real meaning' of words is concealed, meaning that you have to think carefully about what you mean before you say it. It also enables pupils to understand that other languages don't always work in the same way as English – look at 'I've got a frog in my throat'. In French, we say 'I have a cat in my throat' – J'ai un chat dans la gorge.

A simple Web search will yield almost countless sites of 'French proverbs' or 'French idioms' – I like **en.wikiquote.org/wiki/French_proverbs**. Here are a few more to get you started:

- après la pluie, le beau temps (every cloud has a silver lining)
- les petits ruisseaux fonts les grandes rivières (literally: little streams become big rivers) (tall oaks from little acorns grow)
- qui va lentement, va sûrement (more haste, less speed)
- quand on veut, on peut / vouloir, c'est pouvoir (where there's a will, there's a way)
- il faut réfléchir avant d'agir (look before you leap)
- il pleut des cordes (literally: it's raining strings) (it's raining cats and dogs)
- les grands esprits se rencontrent (great minds think alike)

Promoting awareness and understanding of grammar

Grammar doesn't have to be the bête noire of language teaching, regardless of the language in question. Pupils at KS3 and 4 (and sometimes even 5) complain that they don't understand the grammar, or find it 'boring' – often this can be linked to their lack of understanding of the role of grammar in language. You can use French as a way of promoting pupil awareness and understanding of grammar, almost without their realizing it. Working with grammar consistently in French lessons across KS2 can demystify its role and the way it works, allowing pupils to be creative with language, and move away from the more common 'learnt response' syndrome we so often see.

Teaching tip

Don't teach a grammar point 'in isolation' – always link it to a topic, use lots of language the pupils already know, as well as introducing new words to increase their vocabulary.

Use adjectives to look at the verb *être* ('to be'). Talk about verbs, and how they work in English, using a selection of verbs to demonstrate their structure and their conjugation. Write out the whole of the verb to be in a column, asking pupils to suggest adjectives to create a short sentence, for example:

To be

I *am*	tall
you *are*	talkative/chatty
he *is*	hard-working
she *is*	sporty
it *is*	open
we *are*	tired
they *are*	intelligent

Now show the verb *être* in a parallel column.

To be   *être*

I *am*	tall	je *suis*	grand(e)
you *are*	talkative/chatty	tu *es*	bavard(e)
he *is*	hard-working	il *est*	travailleur
she *is*	sporty	elle *est*	sportive
it *is*	open	elle (la porte) *est*	est ouverte
we *are*	tired	nous *sommes*	fatigués
they *are*	intelligent	ils *sont*	intelligents
		elles *sont*	intelligentes

This will also help to reinforce adjectival agreement – show the difference in adjectives for masculine, feminine, singular and plural.

Activity

Now get pupils to create new sentences in pairs on their mini whiteboards or in their exercise books – against the clock works well, maximum 5 minutes, with a point for the pair that comes up with the most.

The major difference between English and French articles is of course gender. I always introduce the definite article with a new noun and the pupils always note the gender in their *carnets de vocabulaire* too. Explaining that there are three ways to say 'the' in French works well – *le*, *la* and *les* – you don't have to explain that *le* is masculine and *la* is feminine at the beginning, although some pupils are perfectly able to take that on board. Knowing the gender of the noun is really important – you're very limited with what you can do with adjectives, reading and creative writing unless the pupils know and accept this very basic rule.

Building a grammar glossary

Activity

This works well for both French and English, and pupils can compile their glossary either in their *carnet de vocabulaire*, or in a separate book. Call it 'la grammaire – c'est super!' – it rhymes nicely, and can become a jaunty refrain, giving a more light-hearted feeling to what can be the 'dreaded' grammar). You might prefer to have these written out bilingually on display. Have matching English labels and definitions:

- Un verbe définit l'action que je fais – je chante, je marche, je suis, je fais, j'ai.
- Un adjectif décrit un nom – grand, petit, long, court.
- Un pronom remplace un nom – les pronoms en français sont: je, tu, il, elle, on, nous, vous, ils, elles.
- Un adverbe décrit un verbe – je marche lentement, je chante doucement.
- Les mots interrogatifs – les mots qui posent des questions! (interrogatives/ question words – words we use to ask questions!)

Start this one off by asking pupils how many question words they can think of in 10 seconds (en 10 secondes) – this might be a time not to insist on 'hands up'!

- qui? (who?)
- que? quel? quelle? (what?)

- où? (where?)
- quand? (when?)
- pourquoi? (why?)
- lequel? laquelle? lesquels? lesquelles? (which?)
- comment? (how?)
- combien de? (how much? how many?)

Teaching tip

Look carefully at different questions, and how they might be formulated differently in English and in French – for example – comment t'appelles-tu? (What's your name?) Quel jour est-il? (What day is it?).

How to use a bilingual dictionary – comment utiliser un dictionnaire bilingue

Activity

Working with a bilingual dictionary can really extend pupils' literacy 'repertoire', and reinforces general dictionary skills. It's not necessary for children to understand how to use a monolingual dictionary first – you can introduce them to the concept of dictionaries in general through a bilingual one. I use the Collins First Time French Dictionary (**www.collinsdictionaries.com**) – this works very well not only with KS2 children, but with those at KS3 too. I've heard good reports on the Oxford Primary Languages dictionaries too – have a look on: **www.oup.com/oxed/dictionaries/ primary_french/** The thing to avoid with dictionaries is creating a reading or writing activity that can only be done by looking up lots of words – this reduces pupils' motivation pretty quickly. However, creating 'speed quizzes', whose sole purpose is the speedy looking-up of a specific number of words, noting down gender, meaning, opposites, or useful phrases, works very well indeed!

Explain that bilingual means 'two languages', and that the dictionary is divided into two parts – one that begins with French words in alphabetical order, the other that begins with English words in alphabetical order. This means that if they know a French word, but are not sure what it means in English, they can look up the French word and its English equivalent will be given – and vice versa – show an example on the board of what you mean, step-by-step – I've tried the following with Years 1, 2, 4 and 5, and it worked well – older pupils are able to do without the instructions a little quicker than the younger ones, but give them access to the instructions until they are confident users.

Example:

Using the French part

I know the word *maison* but am not sure what it means in English.

I go to the French part of the dictionary, which is in the first half of the book, and where all the words are given in French first.

I find the words beginning with *m* by saying the alphabet to myself.

I now look for words beginning with *ma-*, which are the first two letters of *maison*.

I now look further for words beginning with *mai-*, which are the first three letters of *maison*.

I find *maison* and the dictionary tells me that the English word for *maison* is 'house'.

It also tells me that *maison* is a 'nf' – this stands for 'feminine noun' so I know that *maison* is a *la* word.

Using the English part

I know the word *vegetable* in English, but I'm not sure what it means in French.

I go to the English part of the dictionary, which is in the second half of the book, and where all the words are given in English first.

I find the words beginning with *v* by saying the alphabet to myself.

I now look for words beginning with *ve-* which are the first two letters of *vegetable*.

I now look for words beginning with *veg-* which are the first three letters of *vegetable*.

I find *vegetable* and the dictionary tells me that the French word for *vegetable* is 'légume'

It also tells me that *légume* is a noun, and a *le* word

Follow the same pattern with verbs (vb); adjectives (adj), adverbs (adv).

> ## Top tips for using a bilingual dictionary! – conseils pour utiliser un dictionnaire bilingue!
>
> You can start pupils off by giving them *quelques conseils*, then seeing if they can add to them. It works well with older children by asking them to write instructions for a Year 1 or 2 class – they really have to think about how best to use the dictionary, and also how best to explain it in writing – not necessarily the same thing – as they discover.
>
> **Tips include:**
> - I need to know my alphabet, and be able to recall it quickly!
> - I can look at the words at the very top of the columns, and that will tell me where I'm up to.
> - The word at the top of the column on the left-hand side is the first word on the page.
> - The word at the top of the column on the right-hand side is the last word on the page.
> - There might be more than one meaning, and if there is, each meaning has a number.
> - It doesn't matter if I'm not sure of the correct spelling, because I can experiment with various possibilities until I find the right one.

School bilingual dictionaries for older pupils tend to give more information, such as synonyms, alternative meanings, information on whether a verb is transitive (can take a direct object – 'trans.', such as *regarder*) or intransitive (cannot take a direct object – 'intrans.', such as *partir*) and whether it is regular (reg.) or irregular (irreg.). Whichever dictionary you use, there will be sections with additional information that pupils should be made aware of – the First Time dictionary for example has, amongst other things, a whole 'how to use the dictionary' section at the front, vocabulary topic banks in the middle, and a map of France at the back.

Activity

Speed quizzes or competitions are generally very popular, and an effective way of familiarizing pupils with the role and function of dictionaries, improving reading and writing skills, spelling, and reinforcing – as well as introducing – vocabulary in the target language.

Extend the activity to work on English dictionary skills, explaining phonetic spellings for example, and giving 'speed quizzes' here too – include some tricky spellings too – this gives pupils an opportunity to experiment with sound and spelling.

Your first quiz might focus on the particular dictionary itself, with a blend of simple and more complex questions, to familiarize pupils with it:

- On what page number does the French part finish?
- On what page number does the English part finish?
- What page is the map of France on?
- Is there a section on telling the time? If there is, what is the section before about?
- There is a section on 'school' – what is its title in French, and what is the next section called, in French and in English?

Include fact-finding questions:

Example:

Locate the map of France, and do the following:
- List the three main bodies of water detailed on it in French.
- Look them up, and write their English equivalent.
- How many countries can you see on this map?
- What are they?
- Bonus points for listing them in both French and English!
- How do you say 'French verbs' in French?
- Name five sports in French – bonus point for taking the shortcut, and explaining what the shortcut is (i.e. finding the vocabulary bank!).

You can gradually include all kinds of questions and mini-tasks in your speed quizzes:

- Create a list of five verbs of movement in English, and find their French equivalent. Include a grammatical element here, by giving a bonus point for the correct 'je' form!
- Find the English for the following words: rouge, la pomme de terre, le ciel, faire, also giving the words immediately before and after them in the dictionary
- Find the French for the following words: to have, apple, geography, England, also giving the words immediately before and after them in the dictionary, in both French and English.
- Remember to add the occasional completely unknown word – it's a good way of surreptitiously extending vocabulary and encouraging pupils to really focus on the word, and its place in the dictionary – do make sure it's actually in the dictionary first!

If the dictionary you're using gives sample phrases or sentences for certain words, select several and include 'seek and find' questions on those too – for example:
Trouvez la phrase pour (find the phrase or sentence for):

> la salle de bain est au rez-de-chaussée (the bathroom's downstairs)
> il a les cheveux blonds (he's got fair hair)

Pupils will have to work out a strategy for finding the correct phrase – do they look up bathroom or downstairs? Do they look up fair or hair?
Give a word in either French or English, and ask pupils to find the opposite – for example:

Activity

Read the following list of words which are given in English. Work out the opposite, and find the correct word for the opposite in French.
English word: night
the opposite of night is 'day'
the word for 'day' in French is le jour!

big	(petit)
empty	(plein)
easy	(difficile)
run	(marcher)
sell	(acheter)

Tongue twisters – virelangues

Activity

Use tongue twisters as an enjoyable way for pupils to play with French sounds and words, and to work on their pronunciation – warm up by taking deep breaths (réspirez profondément), make an *r* sound for as long as you can to practise rolling the *r*, (faites comme ça, and model the sound) pinch your nose (pincez le nez) to practise the *u* sound in words like *un*, choose some individual letters to work on general diction – for example repeating *t*, *p*, *b*, *d*, *m*, *n* sharply and with a wide mouth, then trying 'the tip of the tongue and the teeth and the lips' very clearly and precisely. Discuss alliteration a little, then move on to practising some old favourites in English – ask the pupils which ones they know first. Introduce some French twisters orally – the idea here is to work on listening and speaking, so don't immediately give them to the pupils in writing.

A simple Web search will yield a fair number of common twisters in most languages – try some of these to get you started:

- papier, piano, panier – or change the order – panier, piano, papier (bag, piano, paper)
- six saucisses sèches (six dry sausages)
- douze douches douces (12 soft showers)
- la grosse cloche sonne (the big bell rings)
- un chasseur sachant chasser sait chasser sans son chien de chasse (a good hunter can hunt without his hunting dog)
- un hibou roux et doux hurle et hulule comme un fou (a red and gentle owl screeches and howls like a mad person)
- ton thé, a-t-il ôté ta toux? (did your tea burn your throat?)
- le poivre fait fièvre à la pauvre pieuvre (pepper gives the poor octopus a fever)
- Lily lit le livre dans le lit (Lily reads her book in bed)
- la robe rouge de Rosalie est ravissante (Rosalie's red dress is gorgeous)
- le ver vert va vers le verre vert (the green worm goes towards the green glass)
- trois tortues trottent sur un trottoir très étroit (three tortoises trot along a very narrow pavement)

Have a tongue-twister competition, either with individual players or in teams – a point for getting the tongue-twister right or a point for listening carefully and spotting a mistake. As pupils become more familiar with French, up the stakes a little, beating a quicker time on a table for them to keep pace with, and increasing the number of correct repetitions before a point can be won.

Have a 'toughest tongue-twister' competition too, getting pupils to write their own for classmates to try – this works well when you make some up together as a whole class first – a favourite of mine is playing with numbers and letters – for ideas, look at the number vocabulary bank, and play around a little – what about: cinq cent cinquante-cinq cinq cent cinquante-cinq fois (five hundred and fifty-five, five hundred and fifty-five times), cinq cents, cent cinq (five hundred, one hundred and five), or: six serpents sifflent sans cesse (six snakes hiss non-stop – not quite the same effect in English!). Or simply take a topic such as classroom objects, and put several nouns together like *cahier, cartable, compas, crayon* or *livre, règle, trousse* – making sure that the French *r* is pronounced perfectly.

Focus on ICT

Discovering France and French via the Web

I've listed a number of good websites throughout the book but, if time's limited, these will give you and your pupils access to key information:

Wikipedia is a great reference source for busy teachers in general – for France, go to **en.wikipedia.org/wiki/France**. Try it in French too: **fr.wikipedia.org/wiki/France**. There's lots of information on the French language too – simply type 'French' into the search box. The BBC languages website is also incredibly useful – try: **www.bbc. co.uk/languages/european_languages/countries/france.shtml**. Try Encarta: **encarta. msn.com/encyclopedia_761568934/France.html** – or in French, **fr.encarta.msn.com/ encyclopedia_761568934/France.html** – looking at French websites is useful if you're making a French language display about France – you can choose some quotes to use in the display if your French is a little rusty.

Your pupils will enjoy **simple.wikipedia.org/wiki/France, schools-wikipedia.org/ wp/f/French_language.htm** – or give them the main page, and let them come up with their own search terms to access the information they're after. If you have a whiteboard (WB) and projector, explore cities together – for example, **schools-wikipedia.org/wp/p/Paris.htm**.

I like this site for a good look at the Eiffel Tower: **www.tour-eiffel.fr/teiffel/uk/** – it also has a great interactive children's space, useful for lessons and in the IT room. Pupils can look at in in French too: **www.tour-eiffel.fr/**, including the 'espace enfant'.

Use Google Maps for a close-up look at where you live – **maps.google.com** – by clicking on your city or town name, the map zooms in, showing the names of all the towns in your region. Choose other areas of the UK to have a look at. Then move on to France, Europe and the world at large – get pupils used to panning left and right, and zooming in and out. Show how close England and France really are, and discover new places both in the UK and Continental Europe at the same time. Work out which cities or towns you have to travel through to get from where you are to London, Edinburgh, Cardiff and Belfast. Then from Marseille to Paris or Nantes to Nice – the possibilities are endless. **www.multimap.com** is another good map site you might like to try. Discover the world in 3D, and have a look at your school and the Eiffel Tower from space – **www.earth.google.com**.

YouTube France offers busy teachers a fantastic audio-video resource, which I've found particularly useful for 'cultural' content. Go to **fr.youtube.com/** and in the 'rechercher' box type for example 'pétanque' – there is a wealth of clips of the game to choose from. 'Tour de France' and 'l'équipe nationale de football' yields lots of interesting clips and information about sportspeople and the sports themselves. I've also used 'les langues en France' for information and clips about the range of languages spoken in France, and 'chansons pour enfants' – which is a great shortcut to children's songs if you don't have a CD collection, particularly at Christmas! I also use YouTube as a search engine in itself – for example 'livres pour enfants' (tips on what's currently popular with young French readers) and 'écoles primaires'. Take some time to browse through the results of 'école primaires', as the clips and accompanying texts give some great insights into French primary schools (including what children think about learning English!), as well as clips of primary schools in other French-speaking regions, such as Togo (West Africa) – and further afield, like China. New content is added constantly, so it's well worth keeping a regular eye on. You may have to try out a number of clips though, as sometimes the quality can be poor.

I find Yahoo 'local' a great time-saver when I'm looking up information about particular topics – go to the homepage (**www.fr.yahoo.com**) and click on 'local' or go straight to: **fr.local.yahoo.com/** – you can search for info under 'quoi?' (what?) or 'où?' (where?) – or both! For example, if you're looking for ideas and information on primary schools in Marseille, type 'écoles primaires' into the 'quoi?' box, and 'Marseille' into the 'où?' box – and you'll get a list of schools, and links to their websites.

An important point to note when encouraging pupils to use the internet is appropriateness of accessible content – hopefully pupils' home PCs will have stringent parental controls but this is not always the case – so you may prefer to guide this particular activity in class, rather than asking pupils to do it at home, unless you decide to ask parents' permission in advance. The school or local authority (LA) network may well prohibit image searches, so check in advance what kind of access you have. If you have restricted access to the internet at school, ClipArt is always a good stand-by – simply adapt the above instructions to relate solely to ClipArt. Before you plan the project work, do a quick check of pupils' home access to a PC – some may not have one!

Other ICT activities

- Have a browse around www.ictopus.org.uk/ – the site focuses on ICT in the primary curriculum, but is a really useful bank of ideas and activities that you can adapt for French lessons.
- Design a supermarket/greengrocers' website or brochure.
- Set up a class or school-wide survey of languages – school-wide will need a fair bit of preparation, so discuss with your colleagues how it may be done, as everyone will have to timetable in about 15 minutes to allow your pupils to collect the data. Design a very short questionnaire with the title 'A notre école on parle . . . ' and the questions: comment t'appelles-tu? Quel âge as-tu? Quelles langues parles-tu? It may be that your pupils will have to ask the

questions in English – that's OK, as it gives them a different language activity to do – translating! Divide your pupils into pairs, and allocate them to small groups across the school, say about eight pupils each, and give them a questionnaire per pupil.

- Carry out a class survey of birthdays, and display as either a bar or pie chart.
- Create a series of 'favourites' or 'bookmarks', of useful sites about France and French, and make sure they're in alphabetical order.
- Create a photo gallery both in 'My Pictures' and 'My Scans' using downloaded or scanned images, and order them into categories, such as 'our environment', 'our school', 'our French class' and so on.
- Create a PowerPoint file (PPT) of classroom instructions with ClipArt/images to teach to Year 1 – brainstorm most common ones first, and add audio files if possible.
- Create a database of 'facts', thinking carefully about individual categories (for example, geography, Europe, worldwide, religions, youth, food, school) in Excel or in Microsoft Works Database.
- If your school has a Web coordinator, liaise with him/her about designing some French pages – use French terms such as *accueil* ('homepage'), *haut de page* ('top of page') *cliquez ici* ('click here').

Working with images

Encourage pupils to use images to illustrate presentations or other work they produce on computer – they can access these from the internet, from their own stored photographs, or simply from ClipArt. Pupils will need guidance on how to source, download and resize images from the internet, so give them some clear instructions – you can build a number of ICT lessons around the use of images in written documents, either in Word, PowerPoint or Publisher.

If you have an IWB, demonstrate the sequence first to the whole class and don't worry about not giving instructions in French, the focus here is on encouraging creativity and exploring the potential of PCs in design as well as working on creative writing skills and writing for a particular audience – in French!

Create a French-themed desktop wallpaper and screensaver for your ICT suite or classroom PCs – this work well over a series of lessons. Give the pupils some key websites to search for images, but let them choose their own search term.

Teaching tip: using PowerPoint

Often pupils try to use PowerPoint as the main information source of their presentation, and write far too much text on each slide. They often get caught up in fancy graphics, and forget the importance of what it is they actually want to tell their audience! Remind them that each slide should contain minimal text, and only in the form of bullet points, which act as prompts for the speaker, and as a visual guide for the audience. The main information comes from the speaker, who prepares a script to accompany the bullet points – so they essentially have six things to do:

1 Choose and research their topic.
2 Decide what the most important information is.
3 Write their script according to the amount of time they have for their presentation.
4 Pick out the key points and write the prompts in the form of 'bullet points'.
5 Choose a PowerPoint design, and type in the bullet points in an appropriate font, and with a maximum three points per slide.
6 Choose a concluding comment.

Fun with fonts, colour and drop caps – encourage pupils to try out different fonts – they choose a sentence or phrase in French, e.g. 'Le français, c'est super!', and write it in 20 different fonts. Change colour, and size, then discuss what looks good, and why. For a longer text, experiment with drop caps (format, drop cap, select style, select font and how many lines to drop, click OK).

Writing in French on your computer

Always encourage your pupils to create documents and posters using French accents – it's a good way of reinforcing correct spelling and writing in French, enables them to read each others' work out loud correctly, and makes their work look more authentic. You can give pupils a reference sheet they can use whilst they are writing – they'll soon get the hang of it.

Try this (also available as **Worksheet 22: Writing in French on Your Computer**):

Comment écrire en français sur un clavier anglais? (How do we write in French on an English keyboard?)

The answer is: quite simply! You can do this in a number of ways, and I favour Option 1 – it's straightforward, and you pick up the combinations very quickly. You simply have to use the ALT key plus a series of numbers on your number pad – remember to activate your number pad first – you can do this by clicking on the 'num lock' key in the top left-hand corner of your keyboard's number pad.

Option 1

lettre	ALT + combinaison	lettre	ALT + combinaison	exemple
â	ALT + 131	Â	ALT + 0194	Pâques
à	ALT + 133	À	ALT + 0192	à la fois
ç	ALT + 135	Ç	ALT + 128	français
é	ALT + 130	É	ALT + 144	j'ai regardé
ê	ALT + 136	Ê	ALT + 0202	être
ë	ALT + 137	Ë	ALT + 0203	Noël
è	ALT + 138	È	ALT + 0200	les elèves
î	ALT + 140	Î	ALT + 0206	s'il te plaît
œ	ALT + 145			la sœur
ô	ALT + 147	Ô	ALT + 0212	l'hôtel
û	ALT + 150	Û	ALT + 0219	août
ù	ALT + 151	Ù	ALT + 0217	où?

Option 2

Use the 'insert symbol' function in Word. Click on 'insert' in the top left-hand corner of your screen and scroll down to 'symbol'. Click on 'symbol' then scroll through the various scripts and symbols until you find the right one, click on it, then click on 'insert' on the symbol box. This is OK, but you can't use it on Web pages, and it can be a bit time-consuming.

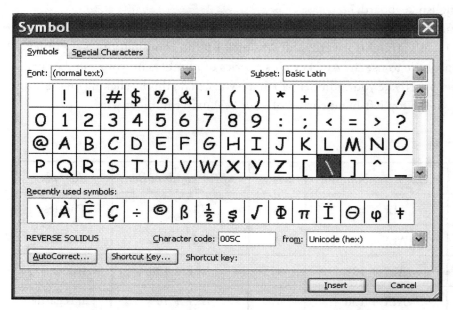

Source: Microsoft XP, Microsoft Office, Microsoft Word, 'insert symbol'

Option 3

Change your keyboard status from English (EN) to French – there are various ways of doing this according to the version of Windows you have – the best way to find out how to change your keyboard status in this way is to access Office online help. Check your keyboard language by looking at the bottom right-hand corner of your screen – 'EN' stands for English. Right-click on the 'EN' and you'll get a list of language options – choose French. Remember that if you decide to change your keyboard, the next time you are writing a document in English, you'll have to change it back.

Create an activity around introducing *le clavier français*, with a list of words that they can type to practise.

Example:

Using the ALT + number combinations, write the following sentences and phrases:

- je parle français!
- février est le deuxième mois de l'année
- la fête de Noël est ma fête préférée

Using 'insert symbol', write the following sentences and phrases:

- ça va bien aujourd'hui?
- où habites-tu?
- bonne journée!

Now make up two sentences of your own, making sure you include at least one capital letter with an accent!

Ideas for using Publisher

Activity

Design an ID card (one page) or design a passport (multiple pages). Start by showing pupils your own passport, and discussing what it's for and how you get one. Include some of the following items:

Mon passeport:

- nom:
- prénoms:
- date de naissance:
- lieu de naissance:
- domicile:

Ce passeport contient __ pages

Pupils can design visas for countries they would like to visit, and include a page in their passport for them – beforehand, discuss what a visa is, how you get one, and the countries pupils would like to visit, and why.

Make sure pupils bring their ID cards or passports to the French Day! Design birthday, Christmas, Easter, le Jour de Valentin and other celebration cards. Design invitations to French Day.

Information point

If you're talking about Easter, don't forget to mention *mardi gras* – literally 'fat Tuesday' – a traditional day of gorging before Lent (le Carême) and general fasting starts for 40 days and nights until Easter Sunday (dimanche de Pâques).

Some Facts about France

Read the following text carefully, then write the answers to the questions in your best handwriting!

France is the largest country in Europe and is situated in Western Europe. It shares its borders with eight other countries: Andorra; Belgium; Germany; Italy; Luxembourg; Monaco; Spain and Switzerland. French is the official language, and there are a number of regional languages, such as Flemish in the north-east, and Breton, in the north-west. French is also spoken in Andorra and Monaco and in parts of Belgium, Italy, Luxembourg and Switzerland and in the Channel Islands, Jersey and Guernsey. Its capital, Paris, in the north central area of France, is the country's largest city with a population of over two million people. It lies in the Île de France region, and boasts some of Europe's most famous landmarks and places of interest such as:

- The Eiffel Tower, called la Tour Eiffel in French, designed by Gustav Eiffel, and built in 1889 as part of the International Exhibition of Paris.
- Les Champs-Elysées, one of the most famous avenues in the world, is just over a mile long, and lined with cafés, cinemas, theatres, restaurants, and luxury shops. The area was originally made up of fields and market gardens, hence its use of the word champs which is the French word for 'field'
- L'Arc de Triomphe stands at one end of the Champs-Elysées, and was built in the early 1800s to commemorate Napoleon, a famous French general. Underneath the Arc is the Tomb of the Unknown Soldier.

- La Seine is one of France's most famous rivers and runs through Paris. Originally it was a key transport route into and out of the city, though now its traffic is mostly tourist trips. There is a little island in the river called Île de la Cité ('Island of the City').
- Eurodisney lies about 40 minutes outside Paris, and is very easy to get to on the métro, the city's underground train system.

The population of France is approximately 60 million, which is about 10 million more than England. The French flag is called le Tricolore and its colours are red, white and blue. The National Anthem is called la Marseillaise. The euro was introduced in France on 1 January 2002. One euro is currently roughly 75p, though this amount can change on a daily basis. This is called 'the exchange rate'.

Questions

1 Where is France situated in Europe?
2 Name four countries that border France
3 Give two important facts about the city of Paris
4 Why was the Tour Eiffel built?
5 How long has it been standing?
6 How did the Champs-Elysée get its name?
7 What is the name of the river that runs through Paris?
8 What is the underground train system called?
9 What is the French flag called?
10 What is the currency of France?
11 How much is a euro worth in English currency?

Discussion questions:
• What other important facts do we know about France?
• What ways are there to find out about France and French-speaking countries?
• What do you think 'exchange rate' means, and what is it for?
• If one euro is approximately 75p, how can we work out what 20 euros are worth?

Worksheet 21.2   *French in the Primary Classroom © Angela McLachlan 2008*

Encouraging Creativity and Supporting Learning: Ideas for Project and Display Work

5

Classroom and school displays are an important learning tool, not only in terms of language learning, but also for working on literacy, presentation and creative skills. I'd recommend that pupils create as much of the French display material as possible, blending geographical, cultural and language elements. Some display work should be created on computer, to provide opportunities to hone graphic design and general IT skills, but do encourage pupils to create art work from other materials too. Commercial language posters can work well, but do avoid putting up those dealing with aspects of French that pupils haven't covered yet as this can often affect pronunciation quite negatively, and doesn't actually mean anything to the pupils. To be effective, display has to support learning, not just look nice and, by creating much of the display themselves, pupils not only contribute to their own learning process, but also learn to take responsibility for, and pride in, their shared learning environment.

Ideas for project work

Pupils can be encouraged to undertake a creative project, either individually, in pairs or in small groups. They can use a number of reference materials: the notes they took for the introductory discussion activity; their 'French facts' book; the classroom displays; the internet; books about France in the school or local library (you may decide to organize a lesson in the school library, or organize a trip to the local library); travel agents and of course, parents, grandparents and guardians! If you have a French language assistant, he/she will likewise be a wonderful information resource. Depending on the activity, there are a number of ways you may like the children to present their work, for example as a presentation via the IWB if you are reinforcing IT and speaking skills, as a written piece if you are working on writing skills, or a visual piece if you want to focus more on art and design. Remember to encourage the pupils to include as much French in their work as they can.

- You can introduce a termly whole-group research project on a topic to be chosen by democratic vote from a number of topics that you suggest – on a sheet of A3, write 'Ce trimestre on recherche . . . ' followed by the topic and hang it in an easily accessible place in the classroom – as pupils gather small facts, they can add these in writing to the sheet of paper as the weeks go by. Towards the end of term, plan for about 20 minutes where you discuss the collected facts as a group, and how you will proceed to write these up and add images to create a display.
- Write a termly newsletter in English for your partner school, create it in Publisher to enhance IT skills.
- Organize a trip to France, including transport (one day, two days, etc.), giving what they consider to be 'essential travel information' such as how to get a passport, different kinds of accommodation available, where to change money and how much might be needed.
- Organize a day trip around Paris, perhaps with some information on the *métro*, such as how much a day ticket might cost.
- Design a flyer advertising a French language course in a particular city or area of France (or other French-speaking region) – what makes the French language so special, and why should people come to this particular area to learn it?

- Write a piece for your school magazine or local newspaper about your favourite area of France.
- Prepare an introductory lesson on France and the French language (about 30 minutes max) for a younger Year Group – Year 6 pupils find this an enjoyable activity, particularly after SATs!
- Prepare a short quiz (oral or written) for the rest of the class (or for younger year groups).
- Write a profile or presentation on a famous French person, giving the reason why you've chosen this person.
- 'Au centre ville' – design a French town centre, which might show various shops, parks and other facilities.
- Choose a topic, such as art, literature or sport – pupils research 'famous names' and highlight one for particular study, creating a profile for presentation to the class.

 Teaching tip

Working on presentation skills is one of the 12 learning objectives of the literacy strand of the Primary National Strategy and French lessons can support this particular objective very effectively. Topics for presentation are almost limitless, but pupils do need guidance on how to create – and deliver – a Bgood presentation to an audience. Advise them on sources of information, acceptable number of pages, presentation (e.g. what kind of book should it be in?), what kind of images should be used, and what kind of design features should be included (e.g. WordArt, different fonts, page borders) – this also gives parents an idea of what's required.

Give pupils the opportunity to deliver a presentation without PowerPoint, so that they can focus on their speech, their diction, the words they are using, their audience, and the amount of time they actually have to deliver. Discuss how and where to stand, how to invite questions from the audience, and how to bring the presentation to a close.

Display work for the school and classroom

- Design a poster encouraging holidaymakers or school groups to visit a particular city or area of France (or other French-speaking region).

- If you have the budget, take pupils on a photography trip, armed with disposable cameras (or cheap digital ones if they have one). Take photographs of the local town, encouraging them to think about why they consider a particular image interesting. Display these alongside some of Henri Cartier-Bresson's work, which you can download from the Web, and call it 'photographie de rue' (street photography): followed by the name of your town – get them to think about how photographs and other images are best displayed, and why. If they photograph people, remind them not to take photographs of people they don't know, and always to ask permission of those they do! Try other French photographers too, such as Robert Doisneau or Ambroise Tezenas. You might like to compare their work with British photographers, such as Shirley Blake or Andrew MacDonald.
- Create a French shopping collage – for a 'healthy eating' and 'good housekeeping' angle, pupils can collect pictures of different foodstuffs and

drinks in French and label them with reasonable prices in euros – first they'll have to understand what a bag of potatoes costs here before they can come up with a price in euros – you may well be amazed at what some pupils think potatoes cost!

- If you've carried out a class or school-wide survey of languages, display the results with the title 'Ici on parle . . . '
- If you've had a discussion with your pupils about why learning languages is such a good idea, create a poster summing up the reasons, and put it up in the reception area.
- In small groups, create an A3 map of France, highlighting key cities. Include the main rivers, and mountain ranges. Pupils can copy from a book, or a Web-based image.
- On parle français ici! (French spoken here!) – pupils can create fact sheets or poster displays/collages detailing countries and regions where French is spoken – it's not only in France!
- Using 'speech bubbles' that they draw themselves, or using autoshapes within Word, link the flags to the languages that are spoken there e.g. *Je parle français* or *Ici on parle français*.
- Pupils create a display of languages spoken throughout the EU, with the country and capital names, and the word for 'hello' for example, in the language/s of those countries.
- Design a European flag display for the school reception area. Label the various countries and colours in French. Show where French is spoken across Europe
- Design a euro poster, showing the euro symbol, and the available coins and notes.
- Brainstorm key French cities, and choose one to create a display about. Keep the display, and repeat the following year, thus building up a bank of displays on French cities.
- Classroom instructions, such as *levez-vous*, *asseyez-vous* – these can be either bilingual, or with a picture drawn or pasted in to demonstrate meaning.
- Examples of teacher-and-pupil target language talk (e.g. qui a fini? Moi! J'ai gagné!).
- Greetings within large speech bubbles.
- Labelling items in the classroom, such as board, table, window, door.
- Label rooms and areas, such as 'Classe 6B', 'Sortie' (exit), 'Bibliothèque' (library), 'Sortie de secours' (emergency exit), 'Bureau du directeur' (headteacher's office), 'Le Réfectoire' (dining hall); 'poussez' (push); 'tirez' (pull).

- *Code de bonne conduite* displayed bilingually in the school reception area.
- Attainment target levels, with 'I can' statements written by pupils.
- Weekly school menu in French displayed in the reception area, individual classrooms and the dining hall.
- Hand-drawn shapes and angles, labelled bilingually.
- Year 6 pupils photograph each class, mount them on display cards, and label with *année scolaire* (year) and class name (e.g. classe 3S); for ICT focus use digital camera, download photographs to file, design display card in Word or Publisher.
- Towards the end of the school year, Year 6 pupils take photographs of all classroom and school displays, and create an online photographic archive of display work across all year groups – if the school has a website, upload the archive for Web visitors to view.
- Create a life-size skeleton, or figure of a boy or girl, and label with parts of the body.
- Over a term, put together an alphabet display to be hung in alphabetical order around school – let the pupils choose the words according to what they know, and can confidently write from memory correctly – use either magazine or Web-based images, or draw by hand. For example: Aa – Allemagne (Germany); Bb – la baleine (whale); Cc – le crayon (pencil) – this makes a great trail for younger pupils and visitors. If time allows, see how many times you can go round the alphabet, but do keep the display up as subsequent years will not be able to repeat the same word, they'll have to come up with new ones, and it eventually builds into an enormous art and word gallery.
- Over the school year, keep track of how high pupils can count – when they can confidently and without error reach 50, create A4 flashcards with the digit and the number written in French. These are displayed from a starting point in reception, eventually reaching round all the corridors in the whole school. To practise measuring, pupils have to stick the cards up exactly 10 centimetres apart (or whatever length is suitable). When they've gone round the whole school, add the centimetres up to work out the entire length of corridors in the school.
- Discuss favourite animals or similar, and create a woodland, zoo, or underwater scene, labelling the animals, birds or fish featured.
- Pupils bring in pictures of their favourite singers, footballers or other famous people, or download them from the web – cut them out and create a 'conversation' collage with speech bubbles – but they have to work out a sensible conversation!

All Together Now!
Tous ensemble!

6

Organizing French activities for the whole school

Activity

An effective way of getting the whole school involved in French is to organize a series of 'French' activities, either over a week, or a day. It promotes the importance of French within the curriculum, has clear cross-curricular links, and is enormous fun for staff, pupils and parents. The time commitment really brings dividends, and even fairly unmotivated pupils will join in enthusiastically with the preparations and the activities themselves. Don't try to organize something on a large scale on your own – this really is a whole-school collaborative effort! When you've got an overview of what you'd like to do, work out the budget in advance – it may be that you can actually afford to do more than you'd imagined.

You can also use a lot of the ideas for individual classroom activities. Give the school a French look and feel – try the following:

- Make and decorate a banner for the outside of the school entrance, welcoming everyone to the event – salut et bienvenue à notre semaine/journée/soirée française! (Hello and welcome to our French Week/Day/Evening).
- Make French and British flags from coloured crêpe paper, and hang these inside the school entrance.
- Make red, white and blue bunting or *guirelandes* (streamers) with crêpe paper and hang across windows or along walls.
- Decorate the school corridors, reception area, canteen and assembly hall with red, white and blue balloons.
- Make it a 'no-uniform' day with both pupils and staff wearing only red, white and blue.

- Create a French literature area with French books, pictures of famous French writers, playwrights and poets (you can find these easily on the internet!); you could extend the area to include other aspects of French arts or culture – composers, musicians, sportspeople, politicians, pop singers, actors.
- Play French music in the background in your rooms – a range of 'traditional' French music, classical music, pop music (search on **www.amazon.co.uk** for 'French music' – this will yield lots of CDs, with lots of different kinds of music – I've bought and used several to excellent effect!).

On vous invite!

Design an invitation in French, using Word or Publisher – get pupils to experiment with different designs, Word Art, borders, ClipArt images. You don't have to limit your invitations to parents or carers – if you have enough room, and the staff to supervise, think about other schools within the local community or local nurseries or playgroups. The French text doesn't have to be complicated: try: on vous invite à notre journée française! lundi, dix mars à 10.00h! Give an indication of what's on offer: goûtez la nourriture française – taste some French food, faites une promenade et des courses en ville – go for a walk and do some shopping in our town, faites des jeux – play games, chantez des chansons françaises – sing French songs, assistez à notre spectacle du théâtre – come and watch our French play. Remember to make a call to your local newspaper, and ask them to come and report on the day!

As guests (or staff and pupils from the rest of the school) enter, greet them at a 'welcome table', handing out the *programme des évènements* – think about charging 20p for a programme and put the money raised towards your French resources. The pupils working on the welcome table greet all the guests in French and ask them what their name is – bonjour! Comment vous appelez-vous? Je m'appelle . . . – and write their names on stickers, which guests must wear for the rest of the day. Remember – all guests must respond in French! If you have time, pre-print the stickers with *je m'appelle* – the pupils on the welcome table can then just fill in their name. You may find things easier to arrange if you ask all guests to arrive for a particular time, greet them at the welcome table, and give them an opening welcome talk in the assembly hall, taking them through what is on offer!

Creating materials for French Day

Programme des évènements

Design posters to display around the school, outlining the programme of events. Remember to add the time and venue of individual performances, and every other activity, like *la chasse aux trésors*, and *le grand quiz*. Recreate the programme as individual programmes to give to guests as they arrive.

Le grand quiz

With the pupils, put together a general knowledge quiz for parents and visitors, focusing on France and the EU. Decide whether questions and answers will be in French or English, or a blend of the two. You can do this as a team quiz orally at a specific time, or as a written quiz that parents/visitors can do at any time during the day. Design and create reward stickers for the general knowledge quiz and treasure hunt – use address labels which pupils can label and decorate themselves – have a selection of praise phrases, as pupils love giving grown-ups stickers saying 'needs to pay more attention'!

Create and display a selection of French-themed screensaver slideshows in the IT suite and on classroom computers. If you have projection facilities in the main hall, display one there too.

Hang word garlands around the rooms and reception area – on A3 paper pupils write greetings, directions or anything else in French you think is relevant in really big bubble writing or in a fancy font they design themselves – they colour in and decorate them, then cut them out and hang them.

Activities for French Day

La chasse aux trésors

Create a treasure hunt for pupils or visitors, giving them simple directions and clues in French (à la classe 4F, tournez à gauche, entre la bibliothèque et le réfectoire tournez à droite, devant le bureau du directeur, allez tout droit (go straight ahead)). Clues can include pieces of A4 card with arrows on, or hints like: presque là (nearly there), vous avez froid (cold!); vous avez chaud (hot!); continuez à chercher (keep looking); cherchez la baleine (look for the whale, or other picture you may have up on alphabet display). Have a couple of pupils sitting at the designated X spot, giving the winners reward stickers.

Le grand quiz

Players complete the quiz, and hand it in to a specified pupil by a specific time. Don't forget to include a prompt for 'nom'! Allow some time for 'marking' – those who answer all the questions correctly win a prize. Add some French phrases to the sheet like: mesurez vos connaissances (test your knowledge); montrez-nous vos ressources intellectuelles! (demonstrate your brain power!). For an added twist, pit pupils against parents and visitors – though the pupils can't be involved in compiling the questions if you do it this way.

Perform a selection of songs and role-plays – for added fun, convene a troupe of singing and acting teachers, and have them perform too!

Bingo

Come armed with paper from the recycling bin, which pupils hand out to the parents/ guests gathered in the specified room – all instructions in French, but do a quick 1–20 in French to recap what may well be very rusty skills! Give out stickers to the winners!

En ville

Create a small town in the school hall – put out tables, and prepare banners with *la poste*, *la boucherie*, *le supermarché*, *le grand magasin*, etc. Make up some street names for the corridors like 'Rue de baguette', 'Avenue grand monde', 'Boulevard des profs', 'Place de la nourriture magnifique', 'Allée' – or name them after *les français célèbres* (Avenue Thierry Henry!) or try 'real' French street names, like 'Rue de l'abbaye', 'Boulevard Haussmann', 'Avenue de l'Opéra' – all these are in Paris. Make the street names look French too – they are generally white letters on a blue background (have a quick look on the Web under 'French street signs'). Design other signs you're likely to see in a town too, such as 'Interdit aux vélos et motos' or 'Défense de stationner' (no parking) or 'Office de tourisme'. Make the café the focal point of the town.

If you have time, small groups of pupils can draw pictures of the items each shop might sell – or cut and paste them from ClipArt or magazines. These can then be displayed on the shop 'table'. Encourage pupils to think about how much these items cost in the UK (you will be amazed at some of the answers, and the pupils will be equally amazed at some of the 'real' prices they discover), then work out how much that would be in euros. Each item can then have a price label. If you've enjoyed playing the 'je fais des courses' game, you can adapt it to your French day. Get your pupils to prepare individual shopping lists for guests, specifying how much they are allowed to spend. They can be given their list along with the quiz, and shop for items throughout the day, working out how much they've spent, and how much they've got left over! If you do this, remember to print out or photocopy multiple copies of the individual items. It's best to play this game with toy or even imaginary money, as things can get a bit complicated otherwise.

If you decide to have a bank, I'd suggest you limit the use of real money to the café. When guests come to change their money from sterling to euros, they must provide some form of identification!

Prepare a simple quiz for guests, handing them out at the *entrée* (entrance). Include questions about France, and other French-speaking countries. Remember to prompt them for their name on the sheet. You can include an element of 'fact-finding' too – for example, 'comment s'appelle le café?', 'combien de magasins y a-t-il en ville?' (how many shops are there in town?), quel magasin se trouve à côté de la poste? (which shop is next to the post office?). Add some vocabulary items – guests have to give the

English equivalent of the shops in town, or some numeracy-related questions, such as dix euros = £? When everyone hands in their completed quizzes, have a 'raffle' – the winning entrant gets a prize, for example a £5 book voucher, or 10 euros.

You don't have to have an enormous French Day – try some individual things first, like the café, shopping in town or *le grand quiz* – which you can either do as a school-wide activity or send home for parents and guardians. Let pupils think of a suitable – and affordable – prize, then have a raffle with all the completed entries.

Au café

Create a café and give it a name. Well in advance of the day, have a school-wide competition or raffle to choose the name of your café. Pupils can research some ideas for French café names for homework (Café Claude, Café Paris, Chez Nous, Au bon repas, Bistro au Coin de Château, etc.). Choose the winning name at a staff meeting or, if you're doing a raffle, draw the winning name at assembly. The winner can be 'le patron' for the day!

Where will you locate your café? The location of your café will dictate what you can and cannot serve – if you want to serve any hot food or drinks, you will have to have access to cooking or heating facilities. Cold food and drinks will have to be stored somewhere that will keep them fresh and chilled. If you want to serve ice-cream (always a winner!) you will have to be able to store it somewhere. There may well be health and safety issues involved, so check these out first – you could ask your Local Authority, for example.

How will your café operate? Work out how many tables you'll have in the café so that you can be sure you've got enough café staff! Year 6 pupils can act as waiters and waitresses – they can generally deal safely with hot drinks, but there can be some health and safety issues. You may prefer to have your customers pay **à la caisse** rather than pay the waiter or waitress, so arrange to have a small table, clearly labelled **caisse**. Don't forget to have a small float of money to hand. Let pupils take it in turns to work at the **caisse** – you may decide not to give them a calculator, but to encourage them to work bills out by themselves (it helps if you do some practise runs in class first!) Decide how much everything should cost, so that you can charge either real money or plastic Euros, which you can hand out to guests as they arrive. It's really nice to use real Euros, and make some money for future events at the same time, and these can be exchanged for pounds and pence **à la banque** – but I suggest grown-ups are in charge of that! Remember, you'll need a good stock of paper plates, cups and spoons, as well as small bowls to put milk and sugar sachets in. If you're serving hot drinks, this may add to your budget as disposable (but recyclable) cups suitable for hot liquids can be quite expensive.

Give your guests a challenge, too – they will only get food if they order it in French! They might need some tips, so you can provide a simple 'script' along with the menu:

Bonjour! Je voudrais un jus d'orange, une tasse de thé, non-sucré et deux pains au chocolat s'il vous plaît

C'est délicieux merci!

L'addition s'il vous plaît!

La nourriture française

Prepare some 'typical' French food for people to sample, or buy either **au café** or **à la pâtisserie-boulangerie**. The most popular are une crêpe (au chocolat – chocolate) pancakes ; un croissant ; un pain au chocolat or aux raisin ; une brioche; du camembert (serve it on some baguette!) du brie ; un croque-monsieur (a lovely name for cheese on toast!)

The menu: draw up a list of snacks and drinks you can reasonably afford, prepare and serve.

For the menu, try the following:

Pour manger (to eat)
Suggestions du jour (today's suggestions)

Petits plats (small dishes)   **Prix** (price)
Baguette-Croque-monsieur (cheese on toast on a baguette)
Salade (speaks for itself)
(nos salades contiennent de la laitue, des tomates,
du concombre)
Salade de fruits
Sandwich au jambon (ham sandwich)
Sandwich au thon (tuna sandwich)
les chips (crisps)
un yaourt (aux fraises, aux framboises, etc.)
croissant avec du beurre et de la confiture
(croissant with butter and jam)

Desserts
la glace aux fraises, à la vanille, etc.
crème brûlée/crème caramel
(you might prefer to keep things very simple – buy a
selection of simple cakes from your local supermarkets
and sell them as 'petits gâteaux' – do the same with biscuits
(les biscuits)

Pour boire/boissons (chauds/froids)
tasse de café sucré/non sucré (cup of coffee, with/
without sugar)
tasse de thé (cup of tea)
tasse de chocolat
eau minérale
jus d'orange
jus de pomme

When you've got the name and drawn up the menu, pupils can design their 'look' and make one per table – have a few spare in case of mishaps.

Decorate your café:
Decorate your café by draping the tables with red, white and blue crepe paper – or if you can get some cheap blue or red and white checked material, this looks really effective too. Hang some Eiffel Towers around the café (www.papertoys.com) and some of the pupils' display work from the classroom. Put menus on the table. Get the younger pupils to make some paper flowers to put on the table – the Enchanted Learning website has some really good ideas for this – www.enchantedlearning.com. Ask your local travel agent if they have any spare posters of French scenes – or download some from the web. Try www.paris.org – there are some lovely images there – including a whole section on Parisian cafés with photographs.

7 Games Galore!

Playing games in the language classroom means having fun *and* promoting sound learning. Games can be as complex or as simple as you like, can have an element of competition and they work equally well as starters, warm-ups, giddy-ups (when the lesson may be flagging), round-ups and general treats. Games can engage children with language learning to an extent that a more formal approach might not achieve. You can use new games or adapt familiar ones to introduce or reinforce new concepts, to revise language already covered, to work on a particular skill or to include all four in a single activity. Think about the learning games you might normally use across the curriculum (such as a 'fizzbuzz' for times tables) – these can be played equally successfully in French and in English.

To make your language games an effective learning experience, make sure that:

- Pupils have the necessary language to participate.
- Both you and the pupils have the necessary resources to hand.
- You keep the timing and pace very tight (don't let the game flag midway through, or go on for too long).
- You are very explicit in the instructions, particularly the first few times you play.
- Until pupils are sure of the game, show or role-play an example of what you expect them to do or produce.
- Always ask pupils to repeat the instructions or rules in English, to ensure they've understood – when they get to know a particular game well, you can leave this step out.
- Where there's an element of competition, you stick rigidly to well-defined rules.

Teaching tip

Remember you can adapt games to work on any topics and vocabulary – and recap the words you're working on before you play the game. The games here are broadly categorized as literacy or numeracy games, but many can be adapted to integrate both! They all work on thinking and memory skills.

Games for games lessons

Divide the pupils into pairs or small groups, giving them a name from a particular topic, for example *les hiboux* (owls), *les perroquets* (parrots), shouting out different instructions for each group – les hiboux, sautillez vers l'arrière! (owls, hop backwards!), les perroquets, sautez sur place! (parrots, jump up and down on the spot!). This also works well if you prepare the instructions on pieces of card or paper first – hand out the cards/papers, and pupils read the instructions. They stop when you blow the whistle, and swap cards. Try some of these as well: sautillez en avant (hop forwards); faites rebondir le grand/petit ballon avec la main droite/gauche (bounce the big/small ball with your right/left hand); courrez sur place (run on the spot); étirez les bras au-dessus de la tête, puis touchez les doigts de pieds, quinze fois (stretch your arms over your head, then touch your toes, 15 times).

Practise general ball skills by giving each pupil a number, not necessarily in sequence (though it's easier to remember if you do!). Pupils stand around you in a circle with their backs to you. As you throw the ball, call out the number of the pupil you're throwing to – if they get the number right, turn round and catch, they stay in the game. If pupils turn round when their number isn't called, they're out. If pupils get the number right, but fail to catch the ball, then they're out too. Warn them you're about to throw (je vais jeter) and praise them when they've caught the ball (tu as très bien attrapé). Keep it going at high speed.

Combine art, music and movement by sticking several sheets of A1 together, and creating twister play-mats with your pupils (for a longer-lasting version, invest in some cheap sheets!). Make sure the pupils understand how the game is played before you design your play-mats, and agree on a series of instructions, *jambe gauche, jaune*; *main droite, rouge*, and so on. Write the instructions on index cards. Decide how many circles should be on the play-mats, and how big they need to be, then mark them out in black marker pen, colouring them in – this works well with large pots of paint – for a less messy (and cheaper) version, pupils write the colours out in French in the relevant coloured marker. When the mats are ready, tape the paper or sheets to the floor, or hold them down with trainers. Play French songs in the background, with pupils joining in the singing. Do some stretching exercises to warm up (see below). Shuffle the cards, and as you call out the first instruction, pause the music. When all pupils are in position, start the music again – they have to sing and hold for as long as the music plays. As pupils fall over, they leave the game – the last one able to hold position, wins!

Bowls – boules

Very popular in France (and quite popular here too!), and absolutely not as easy as it looks. You'll need some coloured chalk, a target, and a couple of small balls. Do some exploration of the game first via YouTube, then create a playing area in the PE hall by drawing a large square in coloured chalk. Draw a circle at the bottom of the square, creating a small area where pupils can lunge forwards to roll the ball – if they come out of the circle, and move into the main playing area, they're out. Place an object (the *cochonnet*) at the opposite end of the square, about a metre away from the top – a globe works nicely – and pupils take it in turn to roll a ball towards the globe. A designated pupil marks where each ball lands in coloured chalk – it's easier to write pupils' names to avoid confusion – the pupil whose ball gets closest to the globe, wins. If you have a number of small foam balls that you can write on, then divide the pupils into teams, giving each team a ball, marking it with their team name. The teams take it in turns to throw their ball, which remain in place until the end of each round. If a player knocks another team's ball, then that team is eliminated.

While you're in the PE hall or on the sports field, try the following: étirons! (let's stretch!) – a good warm-up and cool-down – demonstrating the stretches, call out: étirez les bras, les jambes, les doigts, les genoux, la bouche, le cou. Improve breathing techniques with: réspirez profondément (breathe deeply); réspirez lentement et calmement (breathe slowly and calmly); expirez vite (breathe out quickly).

Another good activity for the PE hall is to choreograph a dance to the can-can music (Offenbach's 'Galop infernal' from *Orpheus in the Underworld*) – let pupils listen to it a couple of times, and talk about the kinds of movements they think would represent the music – put together a dance, and perform it at assembly or French Day.

Draw a big compass with directions on it, showing it to the pupils, and practising pronunciation (le nord, le nord-est, le nord-ouest, le sud, le sud-est, le sud-ouest, l'est, l'ouest, le centre). Gather everyone in the middle, pointing out where *nord* is in the hall – in quick succession, call out different compass points, the last pupil to reach the point has to sit out until you have an outright winner.

Games to enhance literacy skills

All of these games are very adaptable – you can choose to focus on speaking and listening, or reading and writing – or all four! Play games orally for speaking and listening, or simply put the questions on a worksheet to focus on reading and writing. You can make the questions simple or complex, or start off simple, getting increasingly challenging – if it's a 'game' with points to be won, the pupils will really engage with it.

Blockbusters – rayon de miel

I like to call this game literally 'honeycomb'. Draw a honeycomb on the board, or project it with an overhead project (OHP) or WB. Each section of the honeycomb should have a number or a letter. Have two teams, giving each team a name. If you have numbered the honeycomb, you can ask questions on any topic, if you use letters, then choose one-word answers that begin with each letter. Teams take it in turn to choose a number/letter. When they answer a question correctly, they 'win' that section. The first team to win a complete row, wins the game. You can play this game with a noughts-and-crosses grid too, one team is 'nought', the other 'crosses' – remember to number the squares. You can ask questions in English, but the answers should be in French. You can put together a series of quite simple questions though, such as *L* – la capitale de l'Angleterre, or *C* = cinquante fois deux.

How many objects? – Combien d'objets?

Choose two or three categories like fruit and vegetables, sports and hobbies or countries and capital cities. Put the pupils into pairs or small groups, and give each one a piece of A4 paper. Pupils draw a number of columns (depending on how long you want the game to last!) and give them a letter, for example 'T'. They have five minutes to note down how many words they can think of per category beginning with that letter. At the end of five minutes, go round each pair/group, noting their responses on the board. The pair or group with the most words overall wins the game. Extend the activity to include bilingual dictionary work – but give it a little longer. A whole-group oral warm-up works well with this game.

Charades!

Set the scene: for example, pupils are in a clothes shop. One pupil mimes the part of the customer, describing by gesture alone what he/she wants to buy, for example a hat. The pupil who guesses correctly performs the next charade. Write each word up on the board as the game progresses. At the end, give pupils 30 seconds to look at the list, then erase them. The pupil who can recall the most words from the list wins the game. Make the game more literacy focused, and ask pupils to write the words they recall – extra merit for correct spelling and gender!

Don't stop! – Sans cesse!

An oral game that you can make increasingly challenging: put pupils into small *équipes* (teams), and give them a vocabulary topic, such as hobbies/sports. Starting with équipe 1, a pupil in the team says relevant words until he/she runs out of ideas, and when that happens, another pupil in the team has to take over. If the team can keep going for 60 seconds, they win a point. If they can't, they're disqualified. If another team can make up the 60 seconds, that team wins the point. As pupils learn to produce more complex sentences, adapt the game to include sentences, rather than individual vocabulary items, for example: Le weekend, j'aime jouer au foot. You can also encourage them to hold 'conversations', based on questions and answers, for example: quel âge as-tu? tu sais jouer au piano?, and so on – but the responses from a team mate must come without a pause!

What words are missing? – Quel mots manquent?

This game encourages pupils to look very carefully at the written word – great for concentration and reading skills.

Either on the IWB or on a sheet of paper, have two boxes or columns side by side. Have an identical short text on a particular topic in each – with a small number of words missing in one of the boxes or columns. Tell the pupils how many words are missing in box/column 2. They can either give the missing words orally, or write them down, if you also want to encourage them to write in French.

Example:

Salut! Je m'appelle Amélie! J'ai onze ans. J'habite à Caen, une ville dans le nord-ouest de la France. J'aime bien jouer au tennis et bavarder avec mes copines.

Salut! m'appelle Amélie ! J'ai onze. J'habite Caen, une ville le nord-ouest de la. J'aime bien jouer tennis et bavarder mes copines.

Link the texts to a particular topic you are working on. You don't have to use written texts, you can also use individual words

Example:

le supermarché, la pâtisserie, la boucherie, la poste, le grand magasin, la pharmacie, l'épicerie

le supermarché, la boucherie, la poste, le grand magasin, l'épicerie

Make it a little different – draw two columns that have some words in common – pupils have to identify the common words, and list separately those that appear in box/column 1 and 2.

Example:

clarinette, hautbois, guitare, trompette, piano, triangle, saxophone, batterie

flûte, saxophone, batterie, triangle, piano, violon, triangle, clarinette

Complete the sentence! – Complète la phrase!

A game to test the ears and the eyes depending on how you play it! This game works towards sentence-building, giving pupils the opportunity to look closely at sentences, and work them out – the pupils can play on their own or in teams.

Choose a series of sentences based on the particular topic you are working on, and say them precisely and clearly one by one, missing one word out, and inviting the pupils to identify the missing word. Think about what you want the pupils to practise – apart from listening carefully, it could be general knowledge, vocabulary items, grammar points such as verbs, arithmetic and so on.

Example:

Paris est la _____ de la France.

Les couleurs du drapeau français _____ bleu, blanc et rouge (don't forget the flag is called *le Tricolore*).

Vingt-trois et _____ font cinquante-deux.

What comes next? – Quel sera le prochain mot?

Either orally, or on the board, start off a sentence – pupils have to finish it by giving the next word or words.

Guess the word! – Devine le mot!

Pupils take it in turns to describe a particular object in English. The pupil who guesses the correct word in French wins a point. To work on describing skills, give a specific number of 'clues' that a pupil has to give.

> **Example:**
>
> Il faut donner trois indices:
>
> You use it for measuring angles
> It's normally made from plastic
> It's in the shape of a semi-circle
>
> Solution: le rapporteur (protractor)

How many words? – Combien de mots?

In teams, pupils have to list as many French words as they can beginning with the letters you write on the board, and read them out to the class at the end of the game, giving the numbers of words they have in French. This game doesn't always have to be about correct spelling, it works very well simply as a team game, encouraging all pupils to participate in whatever way they can. Before you start the game, give the pupils a few minutes to scan their *carnets de vocabulaire*, and give some examples as well:

M   la maison, la mère, le melon
C   le chat, le crayon, chercher
T   treize, la trousse, le timbre

Quick words – les mots rapides

A pupil says a letter of the French alphabet, and the next pupil has to give a word in French beginning with that letter. If that pupil can't, go on to the next pupil. As each pupil gives a word, write it on the board. You can award points, though this works well without a competitive edge too. It also works well if you let the pupils give you a series of letters – they thoroughly enjoy playing against the teacher. Remember to practise the alphabet first, and you may also find it useful to play the game in English a few times too.

The first letter/the last letter – la première lettre/la dernière lettre

Write a series of words on the board or on a worksheet with either the first or last letter missing – pupils have to work out what the missing letter is:

_anvier   (janvier)
lund_   (lundi)

Make it more challenging, and leave two blanks!

What's the question? – Quelle est la question?

An alternative way to practise general knowledge or arithmetic. Give the pupils *la réponse*. To win a point, they have to come up with the correct question. In maths, there are lots of possibles so you may want to specify if it's got to be *addition*, *soustraction*, *multiplication* or *division*:

La réponse:	Londres
La question:	quelle est la capitale de l'Angleterre?
La réponse:	vingt-deux
La question:	onze fois deux

You can differentiate the game by allowing pupils to give the question in English – just add a bonus point for giving it in French:

Dans mon sac/ma boîte j'ai . . . (in my bag/box I've got . . .)

Put a number of objects into a bag or a box. You can keep to a particular topic, such as clothes (use pictures, rather than real ones!) or food items (use plastic ones – you can pick these up cheaply in the toy section of most big supermarkets), or mix them up. Pupils sit in a circle, or if their tables are close enough, they can remain there, and pass around the bag/box. When you stop the music, the pupil with the bag/box takes an object out and has to say the sentence 'dans mon sac/ma boîte j'ai une règle, un croissant', etc.

How good's my memory? – Mémoire, mémoire! (or: Qu'est-ce qui manque? What's missing?)

A great memory game, which can be played a number of ways. Try this: on an OHP or the IWB, screen a number of objects or words for 10 seconds, then remove it. Pupils have to say/write what was there. The pupil or team that can remember the most wins a point. With this game, give them a warm-up first – show the first screen, chant the words together, then as a whole group, chant them back when the screen is removed. Or try it like this: on the IWB, display a selection of objects, say fruit and vegetables; give the pupils a couple of minutes to look and memorize – you can do this with them orally in French. Tell them to close their eyes (fermez les yeux) or lower their heads (baissez la tête) and remove one object or word from the screen (you can do this without fancy software by preparing a series of slides in PowerPoint); the pupils tell you in French what object has been removed. You can have *deux équipes* (two teams) or let the pupils play individually – the game works just as well on an OHP – photocopy pictures of the objects onto a transparency, cut them out, and remove them from the projector plate one by one. Remember you don't have to use pictures – if you want to focus on spelling and reading, just substitute labels for the pictures.

Make a list – faites une liste

Divide pupils into small teams, and give them a particular category of words, such as kinds of weather, school subjects or colours. The team who can come up with the highest number of words belonging to that category in two minutes wins the game. Give them an example to start with as a whole group – for example 'capital cities' – how many can they come up with in two minutes?
You can play this game in a slightly different way too – the pupils stand up, and each one has to give you a word belonging to a particular category – for example you say *un magasin* and the pupil answers *le magasin de sports* and can remain standing. You ask the next pupil *un animal* – if the pupil can't give an answer, he/she sits down. The last pupil standing wins the game.

What kind of thing is it? – C'est quelle genre/quel type de chose?

This game follows on from 'faites une liste' and, like that game, is good for really working on reinforcing vocabulary, and getting pupils to think about individual words. It works particularly well for older pupils with a more advanced vocabulary, and also helps to reinforce genders – play it orally, or create a worksheet.

Example:

Quel genre de chose est une banane?

Une banane est /c'est un fruit.

Quel genre de chose est le dessin?

Dessin est /c'est une matière.

Quel genre de chose est septembre?

Septembre est /c'est un mois.

Yes or no? – Oui ou non?

Whole group or pairs works well here, and it's good to play when they've got used to the category words in French. One pupil writes down a single word in French, such as *Paris*, keeping it hidden from the class. The rest of the class has to ask questions to find out what the word is, but can only be given *oui* or *non* as a response. So for example, c'est une ville? c'est un fruit? c'est une personne? c'est une couleur? You can also allow pupils to ask the questions in English. It also helps if you list a number of categories on the board that the word might belong to – otherwise the game could take a very long time! For example: *les villes en France, les pays, les matières* and so on. If you limit the number of questions allowed to ten or 20, then the game becomes 'Ten or 20 questions'.

I can speak . . . – Je sais parler . . .

A good game to practise listening and speaking skills, as well as improving general knowledge. Using the flashcards you prepared when you introduced countries, flags and colours, hold each one up, prompting the pupils to tell you what languages are spoken in the country – give them an example first by holding up the French flag and saying Je sais parler français' – if you've talked to them about the various ethnic communities in France, you could add those languages too, such as Arabic (arabe) and Urdu (urdu).

What word is it? – C'est quel mot?

Choose a series of words you want to practise, for example action verbs:
chanter, marcher, regarder, écouter, jouer, faire (to sing, to walk, to look at, to listen to, to play, to do)
Going through them one by one, write *T H N C E A R* (or any combination!) on the board, asking the pupils to work out the word – it will help if you recap the verbs first, and mime each one as you write it. Pupils work out the word, and have to spell it correctly to win a point for themselves or for their team. Alternatively, write them on a sheet of paper for a reading activity or for a piece of homework.

Find the right word! – Trouve le bon mot!

Divide the class into two teams. Draw a vertical line on the board, creating two columns. In each column, put the first letter of each word you want to practise, for example countries. Team members come to the board and write a country beginning with that letter to win a point – you can award a bonus point if the pupils can write the correct article.
For example:

F (la France)	F
A (l'Allemagne)	A
A (l'Angleterre)	A
S (la Suisse)	S
P (le Portugal)	P

Le or *la*? – *Le* ou *la*?

A quick-fire game for practising the definite article and genders – change it to *un* ou *une* to practise the indefinite article.

- Play it orally, calling out nouns – pupils respond by putting up their hands.
- Make it a team competition – with as many teams as you like – keep careful score on the board!
- Play it silently – hold up a card with the word written on it in French – or if you have a whiteboard, with a single word on a PowerPoint slide – pupils have to write down *le* or *la*.

- Play it with a twist – substitute the English word for the French one – pupils respond either orally or in writing with the French word – one point for the noun, a bonus point for the correct gender!

You can use this game to reinforce either groups of words on a particular topic, say fruit and vegetables, or play a 'random' game – tell the pupils it can be any word that you've been learning together in French – give them five minutes to scan their *carnets de vocabulaire* first

I'm going to market to buy . . . – je vais au marché et j'achète . . .

Another good memory game, and one that provides a good opportunity for practising pronunciation and embedding vocabulary.

When you've introduced various words for food, drink, fruit or vegetables, play this game over a series of lessons, making note of the number of items pupils can remember – it will soon add up, and it encourages pupils to help each other remember words.

For example:

Teacher: je vais au marché et j'achète une baguette.

Pupil 1:   je vais au marché et j'achète une baguette et un kilo de pommes de terre.

Pupil 2:   je vais au marché et j'achète une baguette, un kilo de pommes de terre et du jus d'orange.

And so on, until memories are exhausted! Use a flipchart to note the words down, but keep them hidden until the pupils run out of steam, then reveal the full list – keep the list, and see if the class or teams can beat it next time.

Grammar point

If you want to introduce some notions of past actions, this game is a good way to do it: je suis allé(e) au marché et j'ai acheté . . . (I went to market and I bought . . .); add the words *aujourd'hui* (today) and *hier* (yesterday) to reinforce the sense of present and past. You can also use it to practise the use of in order to = *pour* and infinitive verb.

Je vais au marché pour acheter. . . instead of using the connective *et*.

If you are working on *du, de la* and *des*, this is a good way of getting pupils to work on those words too.

Je vais au marché pour acheter du pain, de la confiture et des légumes.

It's me! – C'est moi!

Prepare a series of short profiles of French pupils – you can also do this in the form of a text, with several sentences. Each pupil has 30 seconds to read the profile/text, and then to repeat as much information to the class as possible. When they've repeated as much as they can, show the text on the OHP or whiteboard so that the whole class can vote on how many key pieces of information they've remembered – one point for each piece!

Example:

(Profil)
Nom: Amélie
Age: J'ai douze ans
Date de naissance: 20 janvier, 2000
Domicile: Caen, Normandie
Famille: deux frères, Michel et Pierre; une sœur, Jeanne

(Texte)
Je m'appelle Amélie, et j'ai douze ans. Je suis née le 20 janvier, 2000. J'habite à Caen, une ville en Normandie. J'ai deux frères, qui s'appellent Michel et Pierre, et une sœur, qui s'appelle Jeanne.

Take the workload out of this game by getting pupils to create the profiles or texts as a separate reading and writing activity! Give them the *Amélie* example so that they have something to work from. Revise several towns and cities, names and numbers. Before they begin, ask them what other kinds of information they could add – if they've already started creating their own profile they'll have lots of ideas.

Teaching tip

Use the cards to play 'Guess Who' – if you do, remember that each pupil in a pair will need an identical set of cards. When you're looking at descriptions and adjectives, for example, *il a les cheveux longs et blonds*, *elle a les yeux verts*, or *il porte des lunettes*, creating 'Guess Who' cards can be really useful – pupils are able to draw quite detailed figures, and practise the language that goes with them – est-ce qu'il porte un pantalon rouge? (is he wearing red trousers?) – remember, *oui* or *non* are the only possible answers, so pupils have to think about the kind of information they want, and how to get it! 'Guess Who' is very versatile – use it for any category of people – pupils can collect pictures from the Web, jot down the key features, and paste twice onto a sheet of A4 – print out, cut carefully down the middle, to give two A5 versions. Save paper, and do it in Publisher, and print out four cards on one sheet of A4 – remember pupils will have to cut these out, so it may not be suitable for very young children as sharp scissors are required.

The name game

This is an example of a more 'involved' activity which has both intrinsic learning aims, such as working on pronunciation and comparing English and French names, and sets a scene for future conversation or role-play activity. It gives children a 'new identity' that can be used in a variety of other activities. Prepare a table with three columns, and 30 index cards, numbered 1–30, each with an individual name – for example:

numéro	nom français	élève
un (1)	Faourk	
deux (2)	Jacques	
trois (3)	Jeanne	
quatre (4)	Stéphane	
cinq (5)	Stéphanie	
six (6)	Antoine	
sept (7)	Emilie	
huit (8)	Amran	
neuf (9)	Aisha	
dix (10)	André	
onze (11)	Samiah	
douze (12)	Aurélie	
treize (13)	Shaynah	
quatorze (14)	Julien	
quinze (15)	Omar	
seize (16)	Matthieu	
dix-sept (17)	Moshe	
dix-huit (18)	Bertrand	
dix-neuf (19)	Yves	
vingt (20)	Pierre	
vingt-et-un (21)	Hakim	
vingt-deux (22)	Alexandre	
vingt-trois (23)	Charles	
vingt-quatre (24)	François	
vingt-cinq (25)	Adrienne	
vingt-six (26)	Philippe	
vingt-sept (27)	Farid	
vingt-huit (28)	Guillaume	
vingt-neuf (29)	Françoise	
trente (30)	Imane	

As the children 'win' a name, put their name in the column marked 'élève' (pupil). Explain that they'll be having a new name, and a new identity, and it's all going to be in French! They'll be able to create facts about their new identity later! Pupils choose a number between 1 and 30, and will 'win' the name that corresponds to that number. If they do not like their first 'prize' they are allowed to choose another – but only once! If they do not like their second prize, you will allow two minutes at the end of the game for 'swap negotiation' (this can be quite lively!) There will be lots of groans when girls win boys' names, and vice versa!

Ask for a volunteer to repeat the point of the game, how it will be played, and what it's all about.

As the children 'win' names, ask: c'est une fille ou c'est un garçon? Don't tell them explicitly what *fille* or *garçon* means, as if they are listening carefully, and comparing the sounds to English names, they will be able to work out that you are asking. You may need to give clues, for example: point to a girl and say c'est une fille, then to a boy and say *c'est un garçon*. Do this several times, and they will understand! Pupils create facts for their new identities over a series of lessons, practising Q & A techniques with each other, and eventually presenting themselves to the whole class, giving them the opportunity to write in prose!

Being creative: making a 'talking' puppet

Children may talk more 'fluently' puppet-to-puppet rather than pupil-to-pupil, particularly at the beginning of language learning, and can be encouraged to make their own puppet from an old sock, or similar. This activity will work without a puppet if necessary. Making a puppet can be done either at home, which will get the children talking about language lessons outside the classroom, or in class time if you have the resources to hand, and preferably a classroom assistant – it can be a complex and time-consuming process! Ask the children to make sure their puppets have a face, and some hair. A good supply of old buttons, ribbons, pieces of material and wool will be more than enough to make a range of very interesting faces!

Spelling games

You can help pupils remember the alphabet, and brush up on their spelling skills, by playing some simple spelling games, which can work either as oral or written games. Remember that most of the spelling games you use in English can be appropriately adapted to French:

- Whose name am I spelling? A qui est le nom que j'éppelle ? – start to spell the name slowly, pupils work out whose name it is from the French letters.
- What classroom object begins with a . . . ? Quel objet commence avec un . . . ?
- Hangman – le pendu – do this either on the board as a whole group (oral), or have the pupils work individually on a mini-whiteboard or in their workbook. Let the pupils have a go at devising their own pendu to try out on the rest of the class.
- What's the first/third/sixth/ etc letter of the alphabet? (Quelle est la première/ troisième/sixième lettre de l'alphabet?)
- Go back over words they've learnt previously, such as the days of the week. Write 'landi' on the board, asking c'est correct? Pupils respond oui/non, giving the correct spelling where the answer is non.
- Prepare a worksheet with a selection of words written in different ways – pupils have to underline the correct spelling (soulignez la bonne réponse).
- Spell out a selection of words orally (for example fruit and vegetables). Pupils have to write down the words you are spelling.
- Letter jumbles – you'll need some sets of small letter cards for this and although they can be quite time-consuming to prepare, they can prove invaluable – if you work with small groups of three or four, you won't have to prepare too many sets. Divide the pupils into small teams and give out the sets, having taken various individual letters out first. Say a particular word in French, asking pupils if they have the correct letters to spell them. Teams who do have the correct letters (or recognise that they have!) win a point. Or hand out complete sets to the teams, say a particular word in French, and the team who spells it out correctly with the card first wins the point. Add a layer of challenge, and say the word in English – but pupils still have to spell out the corresponding word in French! Remember to keep careful score.
- Bingo with letters – bingo doesn't always have to be with numbers!
- Prepare a word search (trouve les mots!) with an appropriate level of challenge – remember to provide the reference words at the bottom. For an extra level of challenge, give the reference words in English, so that pupils will have to remember the French words before they can begin searching! Do it the opposite way around too – put the English words in the grid, with the reference words in French. Get the pupils to design one for homework.
- Mots croisés – crosswords! These work very well, can be introduced early on in a language programme, and, like word searches, can be very easily

differentiated. You can give clues in English or in French, either very straightforward clues:

The first day of the week/le premier jour de la semaine = lundi.

Or some general knowledge clues:

The capital of Portugal/La capitale du Portugal = Lisbonne.

Again, get the pupils to design their own, either individually or in pairs.

Don't forget to encourage them to use their carnet de vocabulaire to check spelling!

(Teaching tip: If you have an electronic whiteboard or an OHP you can present these as whole-group oral activities, and so can the pupils, which helps their speaking, presentation and ICT skills – this works particularly well with older pupils.)

- Comment ça s'écrit? How do you spell it? This is a variation on 'qu'est-ce qui manque?' that encourages pupils to look really closely at the written word. Prepare the game as above, but using numbered labels for the object words spelt in a variety of ways, for example '1: la bannanne', '2: la bannane', '3: la banane'.

  Place a picture of the object next to the words. Ask 'comment ça s'écrit?' Pupils say the number corresponding to the correct spelling. Extend this by asking pupils to spell out the individual letters of each word in French. Alternatively, point to each word, asking 'c'est correct?', prompting the pupils to respond 'oui' or 'non' – where the answer is 'non', pupils must offer the correct spelling in French. It can be fun to ask 'trick' questions; ask pupils whether the correct spelling is there or not – and sometimes it won't be – when it isn't, ask them to spell it out, writing down each letter on the whiteboard or transparency as they say it. I sometimes deliberately write an incorrect letter down which brings forth cries of 'Non, madame!'

  (Grammar tip: this is a good way of practising genders and plurals too – is it le banane or la banane? Are bananas les banane, la bananes or les bananes?)

- Comment ça s'écrit? Also works well as a written worksheet – give the word in English with a variety of spellings for the corresponding French word – pupils either underline or circle the correct spelling, for example:

  Soulignez le bon mot!

  Pear: le poire la poir la poire la piore – let pupils create a series of these for each other!

Games to enhance numeracy

Remember, you will be able to adapt most of the numeracy games you play with your pupils for French lessons.

 Teaching tip

Teach your pupils up to a hundred or beyond as quickly as you can – this extends the range and complexity of the games you can play.

We're counting in French – on compte en français!

As children learn to count, introduce 'on compte' on a regular basis, seeing how far the pupils can get each time. Keep a chart on the wall, with a date for each attempt to break the last record.

Odds and evens – chiffres impairs, chiffres pairs

Adapt the simple counting game to focus on odds and evens. Tell the pupils whether they are counting *chiffres impairs* (odds) or *chiffres pairs* (evens). Until the pupils are confident counting in French (which they very soon will be!) make this less of a competitive activity – get them to practise in small groups first. You can practise all together, clapping rhythmically. Eventually play it as a whole-group game, and when a pupil says the wrong number, he or she sits down. Or you can simply write down a number on the board, asking pupils to call out 'chiffre impair' or 'chiffre pair' – until you're sure that pupils know the difference between *impair* and *pair*, write *impair* = 'odd'/*pair* = 'even' on the board in big letters. You can create a simple but effective worksheet to reinforce odds and evens, making it a French quiz, rather than practising numeracy. For example:

1 impair + impair + pair + pair + pair = pair
2 3 chiffres impairs + 4 chiffres pairs = chiffre impair

Language tip

There are three words for 'number' in French, *nombre*, *chiffre* and *numéro* – taking the number 123 (one hundred and twenty-three) as an example, 123 is the *nombre* (whole number), 1, 2, 3 are each a *chiffre* (digit), and *numéro* is used only when calling out a number: numéro 123 gagne!! (number 123 is the winner!!).

Follow me! – Suivez-moi!

Decide on a sequence of numbers, such as 'fives'. Start to clap rhythmically, saying 'cinq, dix, quinze, vingt', etc. As pupils begin to recognize the pattern they can join in. Make it more challenging by going backwards sometimes! Or ask the pupils to put their hands up if they can recognize the pattern and give the next number in the sequence. Supplement the oral 'suivez-moi' with a written one, writing out the numbers in full in French. For example: un, quatre, huit, treize, dix-neuf.

Countdown! – Des chiffres (et des lettres)!

Countdown on Channel 4 television is actually based on the French television game 'Des chiffres et des lettres' which started in 1972 – you don't have to play with *chiffres* and *lettres* in the same game, separate them according to whether you want to focus on literacy or numeracy. For the *chiffres* part, write a number on the board, giving pupils the series of numbers that make up the final sum. For example: 250, with 25, 5, 4, 2. The correct answer would be: cinq multipliés par vingt-cinq égalent cent vingt-cinq, cent vingt-cinq multipliés par quatre égalent cinq cents, cinq cents divisés par deux égalent deux cent cinquante. Remember, each of these numbers can only be used once, and all of them must be used. You can make these calculations as simple or as complex as you like. Increase the challenge by giving the series of numbers out of sequence, for example: 2, 5, 24, 4. Put the pupils into pairs to work out some *chiffres* for the rest of the class.

Fast numbers – chiffres rapides

'Chiffres rapides' is a great opportunity for practising mental arithmetic. Call out a series of random numbers – in each case, pupils have to tell you either the number below or the number after. Make it a bit tougher – three numbers below or after. Or your number multiplied by two, divided by four and so on. This is a game where you might think about allowing 'shouting out'!

I'm always right – j'ai toujours raison

Pupils will ideally use mini whiteboards for this game, or a pen and a piece of paper as things can get quite complicated. It's a great game for showing the class that teacher is 'always right'! Show everyone that you are writing down a number that will remain hidden until the end of the game. Ask the pupils to choose a number between zero and ten, or 11 and 20 and so on. They can use one side of the mini whiteboard or paper to note down their calculations . . . Take them through a series of calculations, for example: *plus cinq, moins deux, multiplié par dix* and so on. Make sure you can all keep track of what you are asking them to do by writing the sequence on the board. Somewhere in the sequence, *ask them to take away the number they first thought of*, this is crucial to the game! (moins votre premier chiffre). Bring your sequence to a close only when you've reached your 'hidden number'. Now ask the pupils to write down their answer on the other side of the mini whiteboard or paper, and to hold them up, calling out the number as they do so. Lo and behold, they will all have the same number – now reveal your hidden number: it will be exactly the same! Of course the key step here is to ask them to take away the number they first thought of – in this way, you fully manipulate the calculation – eventually, someone will spot the key factor in why you are always right – make that as tricky as you can, by saying it at completely different times each time you play it. Let's see a simple example of the game in action:

Write *vingt-six* or 26 on a piece of paper, and keep it turned down on your desk.
    Pupils choose a number between zero and ten.
    Pupil A chooses two, and Pupil B chooses five.
    Tell them to add *dix*.
    Pupil A now has 12, Pupil B now has 15. You have ten.
    Tell them to add another *vingt*/20. Pupil A now has 32, Pupil B now has 35. You have 30. Tell them to take away the number they first thought of.
    You now all have 30.
    You can carry on with the calculation as long as you like, because you are all on the same number – though your pupils will have no idea of that!
    Eventually bring the total to 26, at which point the pupils will call out *vingt-six*, whilst waving their mini whiteboards.
    Reveal your hidden number to the wonderment of your class!

How old are you? – Tu as quel âge?

A number game that's quite similar to 'jai toujours raison'. Pupils can work out each others' ages, and yours! You might prefer to play this first in English, though the instructions are quite simple to follow in French, particularly if you go through each step on the board to demonstrate them. Give the pupils a small piece of paper to do their calculations on, keeping the numbers small to begin with, but building up to higher numbers as quickly as you can by creating different characters who are 'old' – see below.
    Here's an example, our pupil Darren is 10, and was born in September.

1: Écrivez le numéro du mois de votre anniversaire, par exemple, janvier égale un, décembre égale douze.
(Write down the number of the month you were born in, for example, January = 1, December = 12.)

2: Multipliez le numéro par deux.
(Multiply the number by two.)

18

3: Ajoutez cinq.
(Add five.)

23

4: Multipliez par cinquante.
(Multiply by 50.)

1150

5: Ajoutez votre âge.
(Add your age.)

1160

6: Retranchez deux cent cinquante.
(Take away 250.)

910

Ton numéro final a trois chiffres? Alors, le premier chiffre est le mois de ton anniversaire = 9 (septembre). Les deux autres chiffres égalent ton âge = 10.
(Does your final number have 3 figures? The first figure = the month of the year you were born. The second two figures = your age (10).)

This works just as well if pupils were born in October, November, December – the final number will consist of four figures!

Let pupils test each other – give them four small cards (or scraps of paper from the recycling bin!), and ask them to create four characters with particular ages (don't just stick to numbers below ten!) e.g. Pierre, 21; Bruno, 35; Élodie, 42; Jeanne, 16. They write the name on one side, and the age on the other. A pupil comes to the front of the class, and says 'Salut, je suis Bruno, j'ai 21 ans, et je suis né le 12 octobre', writing the facts on the board. He/she then takes the class through the calculation. When the calculation is finished, pupils with the right answer put their hands up, and the pupil asks for a volunteer to come and work through Bruno's calculation on the board! This is a really good way of practising long multiplication, and subtraction. You can do this as pair work too.

Add a twist to things: pupils create four characters, giving each a name, birthday and age (for example Jean-Paul, novembre, 21 ans; Antoine, mars, 18 ans; Stéphanie, juillet, 30 ans; Isabelle, mai, sept ans), but work out the final number for just one of them, say Jean-Paul = 1121.

A volunteer writes this number on the board, and the rest of the class have to work out which character it refers to by reversing the calculations. Remember to go through this with them several times as a whole group first. Let's look at this in action, using Jean-Paul:

1121

1: Maintenant *ajoutez* deux cent cinquante.
(Now *add* 250).

1371

2: Maintenant *retranchez* l'âge (21).
(Now *take away* the age (of one of the characters)).

1350

3: *Divisez* par cinquante.
(Now *divide* by 50.)

27

4: *Moins* cinq.
(*Take away* five).

22

5: *Divisez* par deux.
(*Divide* by two).

11

If they reach the correct number for the month, and can put that together with the age of the character they added to give 1121, they're right!

Eagle-eyed pupils will work out the correct character right away simply by looking at the details: Jean-Paul – novembre (11) and 21 years of age = 1121. Antoine – mars (3) and 18 years of age = 318 and so on.

It's growing! – Ça pousse!

Decide on the times table you want to practise, for example 'three'. The first pupil says 'trois', the following says 'trois, six', the next pupil 'trois, six, neuf' and so on. Don't always go in sequence, keep the pupils on their toes, pointing to individuals out of sequence.

More or less – plus ou moins

A whole-group oral game which can be played with lots of different numbers and calculations. Say a number, for example 'ten', adding *plus* or *moins*, then point to a pupil who has to either add ten to it, or subtract ten from it, giving the new total in French. The pupil then points to another pupil, who has to add or subtract ten, giving a new total, and so on.

Disappearing numbers – les chiffres disparaissent

Prepare a series of number sheets and give one to each pupil. The amount of numbers you use depends on the age and ability range of the pupils, but individual sheets are easy to differentiate. Pupils have about 10 seconds to scan the page. Now call out 'rayez tous les chiffres avec sept' (cross out all the numbers with seven in them), 'rayez tous les chiffres qui peuvent êtres divisés par deux' (cross out all the numbers that can be divided by two) or 'rayez tous les chiffres impairs' (cross out all the odd numbers) and so on. The first pupil to cross out all the numbers wins the game – do check they've done it properly! It's easy to do this as a whole-class activity on the whiteboard or OHP too, with pupils telling you which numbers to cross off each time.

In the right order! – Le bon ordre!

A simple number game you can play in a variety of ways:

- As a memory workout and to practise listening say a series of numbers such as deux, huit, quatre, six.
- Pupils have to repeat the series (mettez les nombres dans le bon ordre), but in the correct order.
- Make it more challenging, and ask them to say the numbers in reverse order (mettez dans l'ordre inverse).
- To work on reading and writing skills, write out the numbers in full, either on the board or a worksheet, which pupils then have to write out in full in the correct or reverse order – some children might be daunted by having to write out the whole number, so differentiate the game either by giving pupils the choice to write the word or number, or give out differentiated sheets.
- use 'le bon ordre' for any topic that has a natural sequence to it – like what we do in the morning – we wake up, get up, have breakfast, go to school and so on.

Disappearing numbers – les nombres disparaissent

Write a series of numbers on the board, asking pupils to add them up in their head or on a piece of paper, and give the answer in French. One by one, rub the numbers off, prompting pupils to work out the new answer each time. Turn the game on its head, and add a number after each response – the game then becomes 'les nombres apparaissent' (appearing numbers)!

Find the questions – trouve les questions

To get the most from this game, pupils will need to know how to count to at least 30. Start by giving the pupils the answer, for example five. They then have to work out how many possible 'questions' can give the answer five – but of course, they have to give the questions in French.

$25 \div 5 = 5$

Vingt-cinq divisés par cinq font cinq.

$2 + 3 = 5$

Deux plus trois font cinq.

Language tip

+ = *plus*; minus = *moins* or *retranche/z*; multiply by = *fois* or *multiplié par*; ÷ = *divisé par* ; equals = *égale/ent* or *fait/font*.

Sit down! – Assieds-toi!

A fun game of survival! Specifiy a number, such as 30 (trente). In small groups, pupils have to count from zero and are allowed to count up to three numbers at a time, but can choose to say one or two. The pupil who ends up saying 'trente' has lost, and must sit down. The pupil who remains standing wins the game.

The number box – la boîte de nombres

Mental arithmetic *en français*! Prepare a series of A5 cards with a single number written on each one – as a digit on one side, as a written word on the reverse side. Decide what range of numbers you want to practise in the game. Put the cards you select in an old shoe box, and ask a pupil to come and choose five cards – as the pupil calls out each number *en français*, the rest of the class start to add until all five numbers are called out. The first pupil or team to give the correct amount of all five cards in French wins a point.

- Make it harder – use 10 cards, or 15.
- Make it a reading activity too – instead of the digit, write the number in full, and stick the individual cards on the board, giving pupils a maximum time to give a response – more simple sums shouldn't need longer than 5 to 10 seconds, more complex ones might need about 30.

Mysterious numbers – chiffres mystérieux

More mental arithmetic! Write down a number, but keep it hidden from the class. Tell the pupils you have multiplied it by two, added ten and have an answer of 16 (j'ai multiplié par deux, plus dix, et la réponse est seize: quel est le chiffre mystérieux? Trois!) This works well as a series of written questions too.

Find the right combination – trouve la bonne combinaison

In this game, pupils have to work out the correct combination of numbers to give a certain total. You can do this as an oral game, or create a simple worksheet. Write the total on the board, and underneath it, write a series of numbers. Pupils have to work out what combination of numbers will give the total. You can keep it straightforward, and use only addition, or make it progressively more complex, using addition, subtraction, multiplication and division. Remember to give the pupils an example they can follow or a combination of examples. Give pupils a number, and tell them that it is the correct answer to a sum they've got to work out. For example: la réponse = 80. Trouvez la bonne combinaison: 15, 10, 90, 45, 20, 4 (15 x 4 + 20).

Combinations – combinaisons

To win a point in this game, pupils have to give all possible combinations, plus the correct total for each. They don't have to write the numbers out in full, the digits will do – but they have to be able to say the combinations and the corresponding totals in French. Give the pupils a series of three numbers, for example:

two, three, five

La première combinaison: $2 + 3 \times 5 = 25$ (deux plus trois fois cinq égalent vingt-cinq)
La deuxième combinaison: $3 + 5 \times 2 = 16$ (trois plus cinq fois deux égalent seize)
La troisième combinaison: $2 + 5 \times 3 = 30$ (deux plus cinq fois trois égalent trente)
La quatrième combinaison: $5 \times 2 + 3 = 13$ (cinq fois deux plus trois égalent treize)
La cinquième combinaison: $2 \times 3 + 5 = 11$ (deux fois trois plus cinq égalent onze)
La sixième combinaison: $3 \times 5 + 2 = 17$ (trois fois cinq plus deux égalent dix-sept)

You can specify any kinds of calculation – for example, you might want to include multiplication and/or division. For more able pupils, make the series of numbers longer, and include addition, subtraction, multiplication and division. When the class has got to grips with the activity, encourage them to prepare some combination questions for the rest of the class – but they must also prepare a detailed 'answer sheet' to go with them.

Allow pupils to work out the combinations on a piece of paper – and encourage them to refer to their number reference grid if they need a bit of help. Make games as simple or as complex as you like, according to the age and ability range of your pupils – orally you can differentiate by giving a blend of questions ranging from basic to 'difficult' and likewise on written worksheets – I'd always present the numeracy worksheets as quizzes.

Games at a gallop! – Les jeux au galop!

Some nice and easy games, requiring no preparation! You can fill the odd few minutes at any time during the day with some of these:

Montrez-moi quelque chose de . . . rouge, jaune etc.

Pupils have to find something of a particular colour as quickly as possible.

Mots l'intrus

Say a series of words belonging to a particular topic as quickly as you can, for example capital cities, but throw in one that doesn't belong – pupils have to shout out the word as soon as they hear it, explaining why it's the odd one out.

Levez-vous!

Pupils have to stand up when they hear a buzz word – which could be anything – I like this for practising odd and even numbers – all at top speed – or play 'asseyez-vous' – pupils start the game standing up, and sit down when they hear the buzz word. You can also use 'hochez la tête' (nod your head) or 'secouez la tête' (shake your head) but this can sometimes get a little chaotic, and it's not so easy to identify who's getting it wrong!

Rub out, underline, put a circle round – effacez, soulignez, entourez

Quickly write a series of words on the board, belonging to different topics – pupils have to rub out, underline or put a circle round a particular word, for example 'qui peut souligner un verbe?' – who can underline a verb?

Le mot commence avec un . . .

'I spy' under another name! Great for spelling too. 'Qui veut être prof?' (Who wants to be teacher?): let the pupils have a go at being you with games like bingo: 'Le mot commence avec un . . .' and so on – you might want to let them practise in small groups first! Start to say or write a word, pupils have to guess what it is – bonus point for correct gender or English equivalent.

Catch! – Attrape!

Only to be used with pupils you can trust! – throw a small teddy bear or similar object to a pupil, saying a number. The pupil has to respond with one number ahead or behind, two numbers ahead or behind and so on. If the correct response is given, the pupil throws the teddy bear on to another pupil. You can adapt this for any kind of vocabulary – feminine or masculine words (or one of each per turn); adjectives, countries and capitals – anything!

Bingo! – Loto!

Pupils only need some scrap paper, on which they can draw a bingo grid (make it bigger for an increased challenge) – great for any range of numbers – to be played at a gallop. Stick to numbers – writing words down may take too long. Remember to give the winner the winning cry (e.g. 'J'ai gagné!' 'Allez-hop', or whatever your *phrase du jour* is) and check the answers by getting the pupil to read the numbers out.

FizzBuzz!

Excellent way of practising times tables and encouraging pupils to listen very carefully – give the pupils a fizz word, say 'bonjour', and tell them what times table you're practising, for example 'three'. Get the pupils to stand up, and starting with you, or a named pupil, begin at one, going round the class in sequence. When a pupil has a number divisible by three, he/she has to respond with 'bonjour'. Increase the challenge by adding a buzz word, for example 'bonsoir' for numbers divisible by five, then up the stakes by adding 'salut' for seven, 'au revoir' for eight and so on – keep pupils on their toes by pointing to them individually. Decide whether you want to include any number that has a three in it – lots of fun and frustration when you get to the thirties! The last pupil standing has won.

High-speed maths – maths à grande vitesse

A game to get the brain fizzing and effective either as a warm-up, a starter or a finishing-off game. Write a series of numbers on the board very quickly, give the pupils a second to look at them, then insert plus, minus, multiplication or division signs, ending the line with an equal sign – pupils are working out the answer as you go along: $6 \times 3 + 4 - 1 \div 7 = $ trois!

Or write the sum out as you go, the longer and more complex the better – pupils see this as a fun challenge. Even if they only know how to count up to ten in French, you can still do quite complex sums, as long as the final total is ten or below. Pupils will continue to calculate in English, but that doesn't matter – they're honing their mental arithmetic skills, and have to give the final answer in French.

Dancing numbers – les chiffres dansants

Choose any two numbers and write them on the board, for example: two and nine. Pupils say the two possible combinations: 29 and 92 (vingt-neuf/quatre-vingt-douze). To win a point, they have to give the total when these numbers are both added (cent vingt-et-un) and subtracted (soixante-trois).

Give me another – donne-moi un autre

With all the pupils standing, write a word belonging to a particular topic on the board, for example 'table', and going round the class, pupils have to give another word belonging to that topic. When a pupil can't think of one, he/she has to sit down, and you change the topic. The last one standing, wins!

Where am I? – Où suis-je?

Write the name of a country on a piece of paper, hiding it from the pupils, who have to guess which country you've written. You can play this with capitals, cities or towns, but you'll have to give them a clue first – for example: une ville en Écosse, une ville en France.

What's the question – Quelle est la question?

Vite! Quickly! – shout out a category, say 'verbe', and pupils have to shout out a verb, keep it very fast, verb, adjective, country, fruit, day, month, country, animal, fish – if you have to wait longer than two seconds for an answer, you get a point – if you don't, the class gets a point – keep score on the board.

Simon says – Jacques dit

A great game to quicken the ear and the mind – it works particularly well when you are reinforcing classroom instructions in French – play with the whole class, and the last pupil remaining wins the game. Give the pupils a chance to be teacher with this game too, as it gives them an opportunity to say things they may normally only hear!

I've also come across this as 'Jacques a dit' – which strictly speaking is 'Simon said', but it doesn't matter which you use. This game encourages children to listen carefully, process the information they're hearing, and respond quickly and appropriately. It's a gift for reinforcing classroom instructions. For example: Jacques dit levez-vous, asseyez-vous, levez la main, hochez la tête, tournez à gauche/à droite. You can adapt it in lots of ways – for example to reinforce colours, call out individual colours, and pupils have to select the correct one from the pencil box on the table when the colour is preceded by *Jacques dit*.

On a scrap piece of paper or a mini whiteboard, pupils have to write as many words as they can according to the category you call out, for example 'le pays' – only give them ten seconds!

Word snakes – serpents de mots

On the board, write out a sentence or several sentences with no gaps
– jem'appelleJeanneetj'aidouzeansj'habiteàParis – pupils have to decipher
the sentence. Alternatively, write out a series of words, either from the
same topic, or for an additional challenge, completely unconnected:
lapommedeterrelamaisonlegarçonlesmathslePortugallesmagasins
– if you have time, do this on a worksheet too, and let pupils have a go at creating
some for each other.